Harper Lee

To Kill A Mockingbird

Teacher's Guide

von Claudia Guderian

Ernst Klett Sprachen
Stuttgart

Harper Lee

To Kill A Mockingbird

Teacher's Guide

von Claudia Guderian

Dieses Lehrerhandbuch bezieht sich auf die im Verlag Ernst Klett Sprachen erschienenen Textausgaben mit Annotationsheft von *To Kill a Mockingbird*, ISBN 978-3-12-578860-2 oder 978-3-12-578865-7
Verweise auf diese Textausgabe werden in Kurzform angegeben:
12 28 = Seite 12, Zeile 28

In diesem Werk werden die Begriffe „Schülerinnen und Schüler" durch „SuS" und „Lehrerin/Lehrer" durch „L" ersetzt.

Quellennachweis

S. 45 shutterstock (Robin Holden Sr), New York, NY; S. 65 Corbis (Bettmann), Düsseldorf; S. 71 The Library of Congress (PD), Washington, D.C.; S. 82 Wikimedia Foundation Inc. (PD), St. Petersburg FL, ; S. 99 , S. 100 The Estate of Langston Hughes published by permission of Harold Ober Associates, New York

Trotz entsprechender Bemühungen ist es nicht in allen Fällen gelungen, den Rechtsinhaber ausfindig zu machen. Berechtigte Ansprüche werden selbstverständlich im Rahmen der üblichen Vereinbarungen abgegolten.

Every attempt has been made to contact copyright holders. Additions or corrections to the names and/or organisations printed herein will be welcomed.

2. Auflage   1 $^{8\,7\,6\,5\,4}$ | 2021 20 19 18 17

Alle Drucke dieser Auflage sind unverändert und können im Unterricht nebeneinander verwendet werden.
Die letzte Zahl bezeichnet das Jahr des Druckes. Das Werk und seine Teile sind urheberrechtlich geschützt. Jede Nutzung in anderen als den gesetzlich zugelassenen Fällen bedarf der vorherigen schriftlichen Einwilligung des Verlags. Hinweis zu § 52 a UrhG: Weder das Werk noch seine Teile dürfen ohne eine solche Einwilligung eingescannt und in ein Netzwerk eingestellt werden. Dies gilt auch für Intranets von Schulen und sonstigen Bildungseinrichtungen. Fotomechanische oder andere Wiedergabeverfahren nur mit Genehmigung des Verlags.

© Ernst Klett Sprachen GmbH, Rotebühlstraße 77, 70178 Stuttgart, 2016.
Alle Rechte vorbehalten.

Internetadresse: www.klett-sprachen.de

Redaktion: Jochen Lohmeyer
Gestaltung und Satz: Sebastian Hutt, Stuttgart
Umschlaggestaltung: Maja Smrcek
Titelbild: Glenn O´Neill
Druck und Bindung: CEWE Stiftung & Co. KGaA, Germering
Printed in Germany

ISBN 978-3-12-578863-3

Inhaltsverzeichnis

Vorwort 4

I. Einführung

Synopse 5
Historische, politische, sozio-kulturelle Hintergründe 5
Angaben zur Autorin 6
Eignung für Sek. II und als Abiturvorbereitung 6
Module und Zeitkontingente 7
Benutzerhinweise 7
Tabellarische Stundenübersicht 8

II. Module

Pre-Reading Phase
Modul 1: Einstimmung (2 Stunden) 11

While-Reading Phase
Modul 2: Kapitel 1 als Exposition (5 Stunden, 2-3 Lesewochen) 12

Post-Reading Phase
Modul 3: Die Themen des Romans (2 Stunden) 17
Modul 4: Lessons of life – climbing into people's skins (9 Stunden) 18
Modul 5: Equal rights (1) All men are created equal – except for those with a dark skin (3 Stunden) 25
Modul 6: Atticus' Plädoyer als politische Rede (3 Stunden) 29
Modul 7: Atticus the man – moralisches Vorbild und Ideal (3 Stunden) 33
Modul 8: Equal rights (2) All men are created equal – except for women (2 Stunden) 36
Modul 9: Final discussion (5 Stunden) 39

Zusatzmaterial (15 Stunden) 40

III. Anhang

Kopiervorlagen 47
Klausuren 97
Literatur 104

Vorwort

Mit Analysen von *To Kill a Mockingbird* ließen sich unschwer mehrere Hauptseminare füllen. Der autobiographisch geprägte Roman, 1960 erschienen, in 40 Sprachen übersetzt, mit 30 Millionen verkauften Exemplaren auf Rang 37 der Weltbestseller aller Zeiten, enthält eine solche Fülle politischer, ethisch-moralischer, pädagogischer, sprachlicher, juristischer, philosophischer, rhetorischer, ästhetischer, US-amerikanisch-landeskundlicher und nicht zuletzt literarischer Themen, dass die Eingrenzung auf einen bestimmten Themenkanon im Rahmen einer Unterrichtseinheit im Oberstufen-Englischunterricht schwerfällt.

Aber nicht nur auf mich wird das folgende Leseerlebnis einen unauslöschlichen Eindruck hinterlassen haben. Als die kleine Scout nach dem ersten Schultag die Welt nicht mehr versteht, hüllt Atticus sie nicht nur körperlich in seine väterliche Umarmung ein, sondern zugleich auch geistig in seine Sentenz „You never really understand a person until you climb into his skin and walk around in it." 33 12–16 Diese Empfehlung ist, wie vieles in diesem Buch, von solch sinnlicher Eindringlichkeit, dass auch junge Leser wie von selbst die Gedankenwanderung vom Konkreten zum Abstrakten antreten. Was heißt es, wenn ich mich in die Haut des anderen versetze, dessen Handeln ich nicht begreife? Des anderen, der mir fremd ist?

Wer die Welt nicht nur aus seinem eingeschränkten Blickwinkel wahrnimmt, sondern die Voraussetzungen des Denkens in anderen erfassen kann, der handelt (im Sinne Kants) wahrhaft aufgeklärt. Der ist fähig zu Integration und zum Dialog. Der kann sowohl die Herzen als auch die Köpfe der anderen bewegen und Verbindungen herstellen, anstatt die Gräben des Unverständnisses zu vertiefen.

Dies ist der Schlüssel zu Harper Lees Roman. Es ist das Leitmotiv, das alle Einzelthemen überstrahlt. Es ist das Sinnbild eines zutiefst empfundenen und gelebten Humanismus, der sich von der attischen Philosophie, von der stoischen Idee der Einheit und Gleichheit aller Menschen, über die Ideale der französischen Revolution und der US-Amerikanischen Verfassung bis in die Gegenwart zieht, wo wir es in Barack Obamas Reden wieder antreffen. Es sind auch die ethischen Grundlagen, auf denen unsere Rahmenrichtlinien beruhen: Versetze dich in die Lage der anderen. Dann urteile. Und dann handele erst.

Dieses Motiv wächst in Harper Lees Roman in jede Faser der heranwachsenden Scout ein. Sie erfüllt es mit Leben und setzt es so bewegend um, dass sie damit für ihre Leser selbst zum Vorbild wird.

Deshalb ist es in Modul 4, *Climbing into people's skins*, zum Ausgangspunkt für alle weiteren Fragestellungen und Unterthemen zu diesem Roman geworden: Wie setzt Atticus das in seinem Rechtsverständnis um? Wie fühlt sich die Ungleichbehandlung von Weißen und Schwarzen aus der Sicht der anderen an? (Modul 5) In welcher rhetorischen (und philosophischen) Tradition argumentiert Atticus? (Modul 6) Woher nimmt Atticus seine moralisch-sittliche Stärke? (Modul 7) Wie fühlt sich die Ungleichbehandlung von Männern und Frauen aus der Sicht der werdenden Frau an? – Scout muss auch in diese Haut schlüpfen, so wenig es ihr behagt. (Modul 8) Schließlich vergleichen die SuS die Verfilmung des Stoffes mit dem Original und kommen zu einer abschließenden Bewertung des Romans. (Modul 9)

Inhaltlich passt die Beschäftigung mit *To Kill a Mockingbird* auch in eine Unterrichtsreihe mit dem Schwerpunktthema *The American South* oder *Growing up*. Der Roman passt zu einem möglichen Unterrichtsthema *Atticus as an American Hero* ebenso wie zu *Human Understanding vs. Prejudices*, und die Art, wie der Konflikt zwischen Unionisten und Konföderierten im Roman dargestellt wird, eignet sich auch für den englisch gehaltenen Geschichtsunterricht. Darüber hinaus lässt er im Rahmen von CLIL (*Content and Language Integrated Learning*) im bilingualen Unterricht vielfältige Vertiefungen zu. Ich konnte der Versuchung nicht widerstehen, einige Anregungen zur Beschäftigung mit Nachbardisziplinen beizufügen.

Wenn die Schüler die großen Hauptthemen des Romans wirklich begreifen sollen – Toleranz üben; Gleichberechtigung sowohl von Schwarz und Weiß als auch von Männern und Frauen; Vorurteile hinterfragen; Verlust der Unschuld; Menschen von ihrem Standpunkt aus begreifen; Leben im Süden der USA zur Zeit der Weltwirtschaftskrise –, bieten sich handlungsorientierte Unterrichtsmethoden an. Dabei steht der Schüler selbst im Mittelpunkt der Denk- und Handlungsoperationen wie Erklären, Analysieren, Beschreiben, Diskutieren und Zusammenfassen. Ein Großteil des Unterrichts ist folglich auf diese Formen des entdeckenden Lernens hin ausgerichtet. Neben analytischen Aufgaben stehen rekonstruktive, explikative, kreative und handlungsorientierte Aufgaben im Vordergrund, bei denen der Schüler erfahrungsgemäß oft vergisst, in der Schule zu sein oder etwas zu lernen.

Beispiele für handlungsorientierte Aufgaben sind Gruppenpuzzle (Modul 1), Kugellager (Modul 4, 6), *posting* (Zusatzmaterial), *Walk and Swap* (Zusatzmaterial), *Maze* (Modul 7), Wandzeitung erstellen (Modul 4), stummes Schreibgespräch (Modul 4), *Place Mat* (Modul 8), Podiumsdiskussion (Modul 9).

Idealerweise passt die Lektüre in Englisch-Leistungskurse der 12. bis 13. Klassen.

Der *Teacher's Guide* ist im bewährten Modulprinzip aufgebaut, aber es empfiehlt sich, die drei Phasen *Pre-Reading*, *While-Reading* und *Post-Reading* zu berücksichtigen. Nach einer gemeinsamen Eingangsphase für das erste Kapitel sollten die Schüler den Rest des Romans in etwa drei Wochen eigenständig lesen. Innerhalb von *Pre-Reading* gibt es einen sprachlichen und einen eher sinnlich-genussvoll orientierten Einstieg; die *While-Reading*-Phase wird von einigen Aufgaben begleitet, die auch während der Ferien bearbeitet werden können. Und in der *Post-Reading*-Phase beginnt die Hauptarbeit des Vergleichens, Analysierens und Transferierens gewonnener Erkenntnisse. Hier bieten wir zwei Module an, die auf eine Klausur (am Ende der Kopiervorlagen) vorbereiten; ansonsten darf das Material nach dem Prinzip des Steinbruchs an verschiedenen Orten angeschnitten werden.

Die Unterrichtsmodule stellen mit Einstiegsimpulsen und anschließenden Hausaufgaben einzelne Sinneinheiten dar. Sie sind einzeln beschrieben und können in Unterrichtsschritten, Unterrichtsmethoden und Unterrichtsergebnissen leicht nachvollzogen werden. Zu allen Modulen finden sich am Ende Kopiervorlagen (KV), die ohne große Stundenvorbereitung verwendet werden können. Insgesamt bietet der *Teacher's Guide* Material für ca. 30 Unterrichtsstunden sowie zusätzliche optionale Gestaltungsmöglichkeiten für weitere 20 Unterrichtsstunden.

In den USA ist *To Kill A Mockinigbird* das viertmeist gelesene Buch im Englischunterricht (nach *Romeo and Juliet, Macbeth* und *Huckleberry Finn*). Es ist aber zugleich regelmäßig unter den zehn am häufigsten verbotenen Büchern in den USA zu finden. Es hat also immer schon heftige Kontroversen ausgelöst. An diesen Diskussionen sollten die Schüler mit begründeten Argumenten teilnehmen können.

Es ist aber auch möglich, mit schwächeren Lerngruppen viel Freude an der Lektüre zu haben, die zuerst so sperrig und schwierig aussieht und sich dann immer mehr von selbst entschlüsselt.

Vor allem aber möge der Unterricht die Schüler dazu anregen, *To Kill A Mockingbird*, dieses Meisterwerk der Weltliteratur, zu einem gern gelesenen Buch zu machen, das sie – auch nach Ende der Schulzeit – in verschiedenen Lebensphasen immer wieder zur Hand zu nehmen. Es wird seine vielen verborgenen Weisheiten nach und nach auch in späteren Lebensjahren preisgeben.

I. Einführung

Synopse

To Kill a Mockingbird ist ein autobiographisch geprägter Roman, der in den Jahren 1934 bis 1936 in der Kleinstadt Maycomb im US-Staat Alabama spielt. Heldin und Ich-Erzählerin ist die zunächst sechsjährige Jean Louise Finch, genannt Scout, die mit ihrem Bruder Jem und Vater Atticus als Halbwaise aufwächst. Gemeinsam mit einem gleichaltrigen Freund, Dill, verbringen sie die Sommerferien. Höhepunkt der Kinderspiele um Geister und Gespenster ist ein Wettspiel, bei dem sie einen geheimnisvollen Nachbarn aus seinem Haus locken wollen, Boo Radley, den keiner je gesehen hat – ohne Erfolg. – Ein Jahr später wird Vater Atticus Finch, ein Rechtsanwalt, vom Richter gebeten, die Pflichtverteidigung eines Schwarzen, Tom Robinson, zu übernehmen, der wegen Vergewaltigung einer jungen Weißen angeklagt ist. Obgleich der Fall von vorn herein aussichtslos ist und die Verurteilung von Tom Robinson schon vorher so gut wie feststeht, übernimmt Atticus Finch die Pflichtverteidigung, um daran ein Exempel zu statuieren, sowohl seinen Kindern als auch der Gesellschaft gegenüber: hier wird mit zweierlei Maß gemessen, und Gerechtigkeit für alle, wie sie die amerikanische Verfassung vorsieht, ist keine politische Realität. Obwohl Atticus im Verlauf des Prozesses hinreichend glaubhaft gemacht hat, dass Tom Robinson gar nicht schuldig sein kann, verurteilen ihn die zwölf Geschworenen zum Tode. Atticus verweist auf die Möglichkeit der Revision. Doch wenige Tage später wird Tom Robinson im Gefängnis wegen eines angeblichen Fluchtversuchs erschossen. Durch seine Beweisführung hat sich Atticus aber den Vater der Vergewaltigten zum Feind gemacht, einen Arbeitslosen namens Bob Ewell, der Rache schwört. Eines Nachts überfällt er unerkannt die beiden Kinder, Jem und Scout, die nach einem Halloween-Bühnenspiel allein durch ein dunkles Waldstück gehen. Doch noch ein Vierter ist in dem dunklen Waldstück. Er ersticht den Angreifer mit einem Küchenmesser und rettet die Kinder. Den bewusstlosen Jem, dessen linker Arm bei dem Gemenge gebrochen ist, trägt er zu seinem Vater nach Hause. Erst hier erkennt Scout in ihrem Retter den geheimnisvollen Boo Radley und dankt ihm. Der Sheriff befindet, dass Bob Ewell in sein eigenes Messer gefallen sei. Scout bringt den äußerst schüchternen Boo wieder nach Hause in sein zurückgezogenes Domizil zurück – für immer.

Historische, politische, sozio-kulturelle Hintergründe

Harper Lee hat in den Romaninhalt viele historisch verbürgte Details eingearbeitet. Die Protagonistin ist unschwer als alter Ego zu erkennen; Atticus trägt die Züge ihres Vaters, Jem die ihres Bruders. Der gemeinsame Freund Dill ist der später berühmt gewordene Autor Truman Capote, ihr Jugendfreund.

Die Zeitumstände der Großen Depression nach dem Börsenkrach von 1929 geben die historische Folie ab, auf dem sich die Romanereignisse entfalten. Es ist die Zeit, in der Steinbecks *Grapes of Wrath* spielen, als zu wirtschaftlichen Schwierigkeiten noch mehrere Trockenjahre kamen, in denen der Mittlere Westen und Süden der Vereinigten Staaten fast seiner gesamten

Einführung

Kleinbauernschaft verlustig ging. Roosevelts *New Deal* ist das einzige soziale Netz, das viele vor dem Hungertod rettet. Auch in der Gesellschaft von Maycomb (das Harper Lees Geburtsort Monroeville, einem Ort mit ca. 8000 Einwohnern, nachgebildet ist) sind solche verarmten Bauern vertreten, so der freundliche Cunningham, der sich für seine juristische Hilfe bei Atticus mit Naturalien revanchiert. Dass diese Freundlichkeit unter anderen Umständen auch in offenen Rassenhass umschlagen kann, zeigt die Lynchszene, bei der sich Cunningham mit anderen Bauern zusammentut, um den vermeintlichen Vergewaltiger vor Prozessbeginn zu „erledigen".

Harper Lee hat den Robinson-Prozess nach einem historischen Vorbild gestaltet: dem sogenannten Scottsboro-Prozess, in dem neun Schwarze der Vergewaltigung zweier weißer Frauen angeklagt wurden, die mit demselben Zug gefahren waren. Der Prozess endete am 9. April 1931 mit acht Todesurteilen trotz schwerwiegender Verfahrensfehler (es war kein Schwarzer unter den Geschworenen; die Ärzte, die das angebliche Opfer untersucht hatten, wurden nicht vernommen). Bei der Revision wurde immer noch ein Todesurteil gesprochen und vollzogen; die übrigen Verurteilten saßen ihre Gefängnisstrafen ab, der letzte wurde 1976 offiziell begnadigt.

Eine weiße Frau, wie immer sie beleumundet sein mochte, genoss gegenüber Schwarzen im US-amerikanischen Süden in den Dreißiger Jahren bei weitem das höhere Ansehen. Harper Lee zeigt nicht nur auf, dass hier vor Gericht offenkundig Unrecht gesprochen wird; sie klagt die Rassendiskriminierung so vehement an wie 70 Jahre vor ihr Harriet Beecher-Stowe.

Angaben zur Autorin

Nelle Harper Lee kommt am 28. April 1926 als jüngstes von vier Kindern in Monroeville, Alabama, zur Welt. Ihr Vater Amasa Coleman Lee ist ein ernster, distanzierter Anwalt und zugleich bis 1947 der Herausgeber und Redakteur des *Monroe Journal*. Wie Atticus Finch ist auch er Abgeordneter in der *Alabama State Legislature*. Harper Lee verehrt ihren Vater abgöttisch. Zwischen 1928 und 1933 ist Truman Capote ihr liebster Spielgefährte, der damals schon eine eigene Schreibmaschine besaß und regelmäßig an seinen Geschichten arbeitete. Er hielt Nelle, wie sie genannt wurde, dazu an, auch ernsthaft zu schreiben. Nach ihrer Schulzeit in Monroeville und Montgomery studiert Harper Lee in Montgomery und Oxford (England) Jura, bricht das Studium aber kurz vor dem Examen ab, um 1950 nach New York zu ziehen und Schriftstellerin zu werden. Acht Jahre lang nimmt sie eine Stellung als Flughafenangestellte an und arbeitet abends an ihrem ersten Roman, den sie 1957 beendet. Ihr Verleger, J.B. Lippincott, lässt sie das Manuskript – zunächst nur eine Kurzgeschichtensammlung – mit Hilfe der Lektorin Tay Hohoff zweieinhalb Jahre lang überarbeiten, bis *To Kill a Mockingbird* 1960 in New York erscheint. Der sofortige Erfolg entschädigt Harper Lee für die vielen Jahre in Armut und die von Selbstzweifeln zernagten Arbeitsphasen. Gemeinsam mit Truman Capote arbeitet Harper Lee von 1959 bis 1960 an dem dokumentarischen Roman *In Cold Blood*. Darin benutzt Capote die Arbeitsmethoden der Reportage, um einen grausamen Mord in Kansas zu rekonstruieren und dann nach den ästhetischen Prinzipien eines Romans zu erzählen. Die damit neu erschaffene Form, die Fiktion und journalistischen Tatsachenbericht verschmelzen sollte, nannte er *non-fiction novel*. Offiziell ist Harper Lee nie als Autorin von *In Cold Blood* (deutscher Titel: Kaltblütig) in Erscheinung getreten, und es ist auch nicht bekannt, wie hoch ihr Anteil an dem Werk ist. Ebenso unbekannt ist der Anteil, den Truman Capote an *To Kill a Mockingbird* haben soll; unbestritten ist wohl sein Mitwirken, aber welche Kapitel oder welche Anteile von ihm sind, hat Harper Lee bislang nicht preisgegeben. Das Buch ist außergewöhnlich erfolgreich geworden: 30 Millionen verkaufte Exemplare in 40 Sprachen machen es zu einem der Weltbestseller aller Zeiten (Rang 37).

To Kill a Mockingbird (deutscher Titel: *Wen die Nachtigall stört*) ist ihr einziger Roman geblieben. Die Arbeit an einem zweiten hat sie nie abgeschlossen. Er soll Exzentriker in Kleinstädten des Südens zum Thema gehabt haben. Die Verfilmung von *To Kill a Mockingbird* durch Robert Mulligan war ein ebenso sensationeller Erfolg wie das Buch; der Film gewann vier Oscars und zählt heute zu den 100 wichtigsten Werken der gesamten Weltfilmproduktion.

Harper Lee soll nach dem überwältigenden Erfolg von *To Kill a Mockingbird* gesagt haben, *When you are at the top, there is only one way to go*. Ob dies der wahre Grund für ihr Schweigen als Autorin ist, vermag niemand zu beurteilen. Truman Capote, der ein sehr produktiver Autor war und in New York das exzentrische Leben eines homosexuellen Künstlers zelebrierte, starb im August 1984 in Los Angeles. Harper Lee lebt heute (2009) zurückgezogen in Monroeville und hat neben dem Pulitzer Prize und der Ehrendoktorwürde der Universität von Alabama (1990) zahlreiche Ehrungen erhalten, darunter den *Los Angeles Public Library Literary Award* (2005) und die *Presidential Medal of Freedom* (2007), den höchsten zivilen Orden der USA.

Eignung für Sek. II und als Abiturvorbereitung

From slavery to civil rights bietet im Rahmen des Schwerpunktthemas *American South* die Aspekte *plantation life, Civil War, Segregation Laws, Montgomery Bus Boycott, Martin Luther King*. Dazu bieten diese Lehrerhandreichungen Querverweise und die Möglichkeit, Transferleistungen zu erbringen, etwa durch die Beschäftigung mit Billie Holidays 1939 veröffentlichtem Lied *Strange Fruit*, das Richtlinien ebenfalls als Abiturthema erwähnen. Inhaltlich passt die Beschäftigung mit *To Kill a Mockingbird* in der Sekundarstufe II auch zu einer Unterrichtsreihe mit dem Schwerpunktthema *Growing up*, da *To Kill a Mockingbird* ein klassischer Bildungsroman ist. Im Rahmen von CLIL (*Content and Language integrated Learning*) bieten sich im bilingualen Unterricht Vertiefungen zu Themen aus den Bereichen *Law, Botany, Biology* und *American history* an.

Module und Zeitkontingente

Der *Teacher's Guide* ist im Modulverfahren und nicht im Sinne eines hierarchisch gegliederten Unterrichtsplans erstellt. Die Lehrkraft kann also nach Belieben auch einzelne Bausteine weglassen, ohne damit das Unterrichtsprojekt als Ganzes zu gefährden – gemäß dem Steinbruchprinzip. Es gibt drei Hauptabschnitte, *Pre-, While-* und *Post-Reading*. Zusammen ergeben sie einen Zeitbedarf von etwa 30 Unterrichtsstunden. Darüber hinaus enthält der *Teacher's Guide* Zusatzmaterial im Umfang von etwa 20 Unterrichtsstunden, die sich entweder anbieten, weil sie einen besonderen emotionalen Zugang zum Thema eröffnen (gemeinsam Gekochtes und Gebackenes verzehren und dazu Präsentationen angucken; Spiele), oder weil sie über die Anforderung der Kultusbehörden weit hinausgehen, aber dennoch interessante und nachhaltig wirkende Unterrichtsstunden versprechen. Diese Module sind grau hinterlegt und können nach Belieben eingefügt werden.

Während Sie die Reihenfolge *Pre-, While-* und *Post-Reading* beibehalten sollten, können Sie innerhalb der Module problemlos Themen auslassen. Sollten Sie sich entscheiden, die Klausuren schreiben zu lassen, die am Ende beigefügt sind, empfiehlt es sich, die darauf vorbereitenden Module in vollem Umfang zu unterrichten.

Benutzerhinweise

Der *Teacher's Guide* liefert dem Lehrer Stundenvorbereitungen, die für eine bzw. zwei 45-Minuten-Unterrichtsstunden gedacht sind. Die Stundenvorbereitungen enthalten sowohl didaktisch-methodische Hinweise als auch Leitfragen und Verweise auf Kopiervorlagen (KV) im Anhang.
Die beiden Klausuren könnte man ebenfalls von der Kopiervorlage übernehmen. Sie enthalten jeweils die Anforderungsprofile *Comprehension – Analysis – Comment*. Der letzte Schritt, *Comment/Evaluation* stellt in höherem Maße eine kreative Eigenleistung der Schüler dar, wie sie auch im Abitur gefordert wird. Zu allen Klausurfragen gibt es Antwortskizzen, die Grundlage eines Bewertungsschemas sein können.

Die Internetlinks haben wir nach bestem Wissen aufgeführt, wohl wissend, dass sie sich schnell ändern können. Für die Inhalte, auf die in den Links verwiesen sind, ist der Ernst Klett Verlag weder juristisch noch inhaltlich verantwortlich.

Tabellarische Stundenübersicht

Auf den folgenden Seiten finden Sie eine mögliche Stundenübersicht, in drei Haupt-Unterrichtsphasen gegliedert. Soweit Methoden aus dem handlungsorientierten Sprachunterricht verwendet werden, sind sie hinreichend ausführlich beschrieben (Gruppenpuzzle; Schreibkonferenz; *Maze; Mingling; Walk and Swap*).

Die Abkürzungen bedeuten:
UG: Unterrichtsgespräch;
GA: Gruppenarbeit;
EA: Einzelarbeit;
PA: Partnerarbeit;
KV: Kopiervorlage;
OHP: Overheadprojektor.

Die Tabelle enthält jeweils Angaben zum Zeitbedarf der Module, zu den behandelten Kapiteln, zum Unterrichtsinhalt bzw. -ziel, dem Unterrichtsgegenstand und der Unterrichtsmethode. Häufig wird als Unterrichtsgegenstand eine numerierte Kopiervorlage vorgeschlagen, die Sie im Anhang finden.
Das Material ist auf 30 Unterrichtsstunden berechnet; damit lässt sich das Thema umfassend erarbeiten. Die grau hinterlegten Unterrichtsstunden sind Zusatzmaterial (15 Stunden Zusatzmaterial + 6 CLIL-Stunden), das an dieser Stelle in den Unterrichtsablauf passen würde. Es geht curricular über den geforderten Inhalt hinaus, ist aber atmosphärisch lohnend. Natürlich kann man auch graue *und* weiße Stunden mischen und dafür andere auslassen.

Stundenübersicht

▭ = fakultative Zusatzstunden

Pre-Reading Phase   Modul 1   Einstimmung

Dauer	Chapter	Unterrichtsinhalt /Ziel	Unterrichtsgegenstand	Unterrichtsmethode
2	–	**Literaturfreier Einstieg** Sinnlich-emotionalen Zugang zum Leben im US-Süden in den 1930er Jahren gewinnen.	KV 1 *Recipe Crackling Bread* KV 2 *Recipe Ambrosia* KV 3 *Recipe Pound Cake* KV 4.1, 4.2 *Presentations*	Vorbereitete Speisen gemeinsam verzehren; dazu [PowerPoint-] Präsentationen zu diversen Hintergrundthemen ansehen und anhören

While-Reading Phase   Modul 2   Kapitel 1 als Exposition

Dauer	Chapter	Unterrichtsinhalt /Ziel	Unterrichtsgegenstand	Unterrichtsmethode
2-3 Wochen	2-31	**Reading Tasks** Sicherung des Textverständnisses durch diverse Leseaufträge.	KV 5.1, 5.2 *Reading Log* KV 6.1-6.5 *Check Yourself Questions* KV 7.1, 7.2 *Road Map*	
2	1	**Grundlagen des *Plots* im 1. Kapitel** Thematische Einstimmung erreichen.	KV 8.1, 8.2 *Group Puzzle about chapter 1*	Gruppenpuzzle mit Experten
1	1	**Erste Charakterisierung der Hauptpersonen** Personen und Abhängigkeiten analysieren. – Glaubwürdigkeitsskala erstellen.	KV 9 *Characters in Chapter 1*	Erarbeitung der Charaktere in PA oder EA
2	1	**Stilmittel analysieren und erklären**	KV 10 *Analysing literary means in chapter 1*	Leseaufträge als PA

Post-Reading Phase   Modul 3   Die Themen des Romans

Dauer	Chapter	Unterrichtsinhalt /Ziel	Unterrichtsgegenstand	Unterrichtsmethode
2	alle	**Auswertung der Leseaufträge** Sicherung des Inhalts; Erkennen der Hauptthemen des Romans.	KV 5 *Reading Log* KV 6 *Check Yourself Questions*	GA; UG
1		**Monroeville – Maycomb: Fiktion und Realität** Ortskenntnis und emotionale Bindung an den Ort entwickeln.	KV 7 *Road Map*	EA; Karte beschriften

Modul 4   Lessons of life – climbing into people's skins

Dauer	Chapter	Unterrichtsinhalt /Ziel	Unterrichtsgegenstand	Unterrichtsmethode
2	alle	**31 Kapitel als Lebenslektionen für Scout** Die Grundstruktur des Romans erkennen.	KV 5 *Reading Log*	PA; Wandzeitung erstellen; UG
1	alle	**Scout gewinnt Verständnis für Toms Lebenssituation** Scouts Ausgangshaltung erarbeiten und erkennen, inwiefern sich diese im Laufe des Buches ändert.	KV 11 *Understanding Tom's situation*	GA mit anschließender Präsentation
1	15	**Lynchmord** Billie Holidays Lied *Strange Fruit* im Kontext der historischen Lynchjustiz analysieren.	KV 12.1 *Strange Fruit* (Foto) KV 12.2 *Strange Fruit* (Text) (Video)	EA/PA Hintergrundrecherche
2	15	**Die Mob-Szene als Lehrstunde** Den Umschwung analysieren.		PA, UG

Stundenübersicht

2	alle	**Scout gewinnt Verständnis für Boo Radley** Erkennen, dass die ‚Menschwerdung' Boos eine Metapher für das Heranwachsen Scouts ist.		UG; Pantomime; UG (Analyse)
1	19	**Scout versteht den Staatsanwalt** Verstehen, wie Dill und Scout das Kreuzverhör unterschiedlich wahrnehmen.	KV 13 *Is Mr Gilmore a fair prosecutor?*	Kugellagerdiskussion der zwei Sichtweisen des Kreuzverhörs – Dills Seite – Scouts Seite
2	alle	**Der Klatschtante die Stirn bieten** Sich Klatschmäulern gegenüber höflich und bestimmt verhalten.		Stummes Schreibgespräch; Wandzeitung erstellen

Modul 5   Equal rights (1) All men are created equal – except for those with a dark skin

1	alle	**Myth-and-Witchcraft stories** Erkennen, dass Aberglaube und Mystizismus sich nicht auf Schwarze beschränken und heute noch gültig sind.	KV 14 *Adventures of Huckleberry Finn – myths and witchcraft* KV 15 *Myths – find examples in Mockingbird* KV 16 *Modern myths*	Gruppenpuzzle mit Experten
2		**Rassismus in den USA – Der Sklavenstaat und sein Vermächtnis** Einzelaspekte der Rassendiskriminierung am Beispiel der Lebenssituationen von Schwarzen von 1852 bis 1939 verstehen und einordnen.	KV 17.1, 17.2, 17.3 *Racial Segregation* KV 18.1, 18.2 *Uncle Tom's Cabin, Ch. XII*	Kugellager; Rassentrennung an Beispielen darstellen;
1		**Die Bürgerrechtsbewegung** Stufen des Kampfes um Gleichberechtigung erkennen und einordnen.	KV 19 *Steps in the Civil Rights Movement*	Zu Hause vorbereiten; Einzelthemen vortragen und diskutieren

Modul 6   Atticus' Plädoyer als politische Rede

2		**Gettysburg Address (Lincoln 19.11.1863)** Wichtige rhetorische Elemente zeigen und das Thema erkennen.	KV 20 *How to analyse the elements of a political speech* KV 21 *Gettysburg Address*	EA; Kugellager; PA; UG
2	20	**Martin Luther King's Speech *I have a Dream*** Funktion der Redemittel darstellen und den Bezug auf große amerikanischen Themen erkennen.	KV 22.1, 22.2 *I have a dream*	GA, Berichte aus den Gruppen unter Berücksichtigung der anderen Gruppenergebnisse
1	chapter 20, 224 1 – 227 13	**Atticus' Plädoyer** In den rhetorischen Mitteln seines Plädoyers die Verwandtschaft zu politischen Reden erkennen.		Kugellager
1		**Spiel: *Just a minute*** Eigene Rede nach festgelegten Regeln und Themen halten.		Redewettbewerb, je 4 TN

Stundenübersicht

Modul 7 — Atticus the man – moralisches Vorbild und Ideal

2	alle	**Charakterisierung der Figur Atticus Finch** Die Person Atticus aus der Sicht der anderen Protagonisten ausleuchten.	KV 23 *Atticus's personality traits*	GA; Podiumsdiskussion
1	alle	**Atticus' choices** Erkennen, dass Atticus in seiner Vorbildfunktion im Roman wenig Handlungsalternativen hat.		GA
1		**Lobrede auf Atticus halten** Gemeinsames Erarbeiten einer Lobrede, wie sie in angelsächsischen Ländern gehalten wird.	KV 24 *Eulogy on Atticus*	UG; EA; kurze Rede halten

Modul 8 — Equal rights (2) – All men are created equal – except for women

1	alle	**Frauenrollen im amerikanischen Süden** Elemente und Aspekte der Mädchenerziehung in den 1930er Jahren erkennen.	KV 25 *Role models for Southern ladies*	UG; GA/*Place mats*
1	alle	**Das Frauenbild im Roman** Entwicklungsstufen von Scouts sexueller Identität nachzeichnen.	KV 26 *Stages of Scouts sexual identity*	GA/*Place mats*; UG

Modul 9 — Final discussion

4-5	alle	**Der verfilmte Roman** Beurteilen und begründen können, ob die Filmversion dem Roman kongenial ist.	DVD *To Kill a Mockingbird* KV 27 *Viewing Log*	*Viewing log*
1	alle	**Abschlussdiskussion** Themen des Romans bewerten und die Wirkung der Lektüre auf einen selbst darlegen.	KV 28 *Topics for a panel discussion*	Podiumsdiskussion

Zusatzmaterial

2	alle	**Rezeptionsgeschichte** Reaktionen auf das Buch analysieren. Erarbeiten unterschiedlicher Positionen.	KV 29 *Harper Lee's novel is a racist morality tale* – by Fred Leebron, Sept 14, 2007; KV 30 *Walk and Swap – Leebron's Arguments*	UG; *Walk and Swap*; *Posting*
1		**Implizite Bedeutungen von Namen** Namen als literarisches Ausdrucksmittel erkennen.	KV 31.1, 31.2 *What's in a name?*	Online-Recherche; UG
1		**Symbole und Metaphern analysieren** Die Wirkung von Symbolen und Metaphern erkennen.	KV 32.1, 32.2 *Symbols and metaphors*	Partnerarbeit
1		**Kreative Zusatzaufgaben erstellen**		Kreatives Schreiben
2		**CLIL-Material Biologieunterricht** Im Roman erwähnte Bezüge zu Flora und Fauna klären.	KV 33.1, 33.2 *Flora and fauna in To Kill a Mockingbird*	Präsentationen (GA)
2		**CLIL-Material Gemeinschaftskunde** Rechtsbezüge im Roman klären.	KV 34.1, 34.2, 34.3 *Legal terminology in To Kill a Mockingbird*	Präsentationen (GA)
2		**CLIL-Material Geschichte** Historische Bezüge im Roman klären.		Präsentationen (GA)
4		**I, Too, Sing America Harlem** *(Langston Hughes)*, Interpretation der Gedichte	KV 35.1, 35.2, 35.3	Präsentationen (GA) *Think-Pair-Share*

Klausuren

		Klausur A		
		Klausur B		

II. Module
Pre-Reading Phase

Modul 1 Einstimmung (2 Stunden)

Lernziel

Sinnlich-emotionalen Zugang zum Leben im US-Süden in den 1930er Jahren gewinnen.

Thema: Enjoy Life in the South

Als Einstieg in die Analyse von Harper Lees *To Kill a Mockingbird* bietet sich an, die Schüler am Lebensgefühl des Südens teilhaben zu lassen. Der amerikanische Süden wird ja nicht in Bausch und Bogen verurteilt; es handelt sich um eine Kulturgesellschaft, deren Verdienste auch herausgearbeitet werden sollen. Ihre dunkle Seite, die Fortdauer der Rassendiskriminierung, ist nicht alles, was es zum Thema „Süden" zu sagen gibt. Gäbe es keine positive Seite, würden wir uns kaum mit dem „Süden" beschäftigen.

Diese Stunde erfordert ein wenig Vorbereitung. Alle sollten Teller, Dessertschüsselchen, Messer, Gabel, Löffel und einen Becher mitbringen. Einige Schülerinnen/Schüler (S) decken das Büffet auf einer weißen Tischdecke, dekorieren es mit USA-Flaggen und bauen die Speisen auf. Andere SuS erhalten eine Woche zuvor Rezepte, die sie zu zweit backen oder zubereiten: **KV 1** *Recipe Crackling Bread* (ein herzhaftes Gericht, vergleichbar mit Quiche Lorraine, aber mit trockener Oberfläche); **KV 2** *Recipe Ambrosia* (ein Obstsalat aus Apfelsinen, Ananas und Kokosflocken) ebenfalls für Kochanfänger/innen geeignet und noch leichter zuzubereiten, weil nichts gekocht wird; **KV 3** *Recipe Pound Cake* für Backanfänger/innen (ein einfacher Rührteig in Kastenform, sehr schmackhaft und sättigend); Wer diesen Ansatz vertiefen will, findet Rezepte zu *Taffy*, *Hot Chocolate* und sogar *Pig's Knuckles* im Internet. Sobald das Büffet eröffnet ist, dürfen die Speisen verzehrt werden.

Für sehr ambitionierte Konditor/innen wollte ich ursprünglich noch ein *Lane Cake*-Rezept beifügen, aber es ist zu schwer. Man stelle sich eine Schwarzwälder Kirschtorte vor, die in 5 Schichten mit jeweils wechselnder Cremefüllung aufgebaut ist. Obenauf ist eine Art Obsttortendeckel und rings herum eine satte weiße Cremeschicht. Kein Wunder, dass die ambitionierten Damen des Südens in einem guten *Lane Cake* erkannten, welche Charakterqualitäten die Köchin besaß. Wer es trotzdem probieren will, findet im Internet reichlich Anregungen. Im Buch kommt es auf **81** 29 vor. Miss Maudie hütet ihr Erfolgsrezept seit dreißig Jahren vor der eifersüchtigen Miss Stephanie! Und selbst die Tatsache, dass Miss Maudie, nachdem ihr Haus abgebrannt ist, bei Miss Stephanie wohnen darf, ist noch lange kein Grund, ihr das Rezept preiszugeben.

Der Süden ist die Gegend des genussvollen Essens. Wenn zur ersten Stunde *Crackling Bread, Ambrosia*, ein *Pound Cake*, (vielleicht sogar doch ein *Lane Cake*), auf einem Büffet aufgebaut und zu probieren sind, werden alle begeistert sein.

Das Lesen und Dechiffrieren von englischsprachigen Kochrezepten ist eine Kunst für sich. Es gibt eine Menge umzurechnen. Die SuS sollten wissen, dass es bestimmte *measuring cups* gibt, deren Volumen vorgegeben ist; *teaspoon* und Teelöffel entsprechen sich ungefähr (doch auch hierfür gibt es spezielle Messlöffel); die Backtemperaturen mit Werten über 400°F(ahrenheit) irritieren auch zunächst. Schließlich sind viele Rezepte mit *cups* oder *oz* statt in Gramm angegeben. Das alles macht ein erstes Backen mit englischen Rezepten zu einer komplexen Aufgabe. Ich halte es aber für eine sinnvolle Horizonterweiterung. Jede Köchin/jeder Koch sollte bei der Büffeteröffnung kurz berichten, wie das Kochen oder Backen verlaufen ist und welchen Bezug das Rezept zu *To Kill a Mockingbird* hat.

Andere SuS bereiten kurze Präsentationen vor. Wer mit PowerPoint arbeiten kann, hat es einfacher als jemand, der Einzelfolien für den OHP vorbereitet. Die **KV 4** *Presentations* geben Anregungen, wovon diese Präsentationen handeln könnten. Das ganze Buch, aber besonders das erste Kapitel ist so voller Anspielungen und Details mit starkem visuellen Charakter, dass es sich lohnt, diese verbalen Hinweise auch als optische Bilder zu präsentieren.

Die Präsentationen erfüllen Hintergrundereignisse (*Civil War, Great Depression, Roosevelt*, Arbeitslosigkeit, *WPA=Work Progress Administration, Prohibition*, Pflanzen, Tiere und Bilder vom Alltag in den 30er Jahren) mit authentischem Leben. Auch über Harper Lee kann kurz berichtet werden. Die SuS präsentieren nacheinander jeweils ca. 10 Begriffe und zeigen sie im Bild. Dadurch gesellt sich zur sinnlich-oralen die sinnlich-visuelle Einstimmung.

Die PowerPoint-Präsentationen sollten schon vorher auf dem betreffenden Computer eingespeichert und in die richtige Reihenfolge gebracht werden, damit man sie nur noch anklicken muss.

Impuls

We will begin our work on <u>To Kill a Mockingbird</u> by enjoying life together as one might have enjoyed it in the South of the 1930s. However, there is a dark side to that kind of life, too, as you will see. But first of all, let's eat some of the dishes – can the ones who made them tell us what they are and how they did it? – and listen to your presentations.

Modul 2

Methode

Darüber hinaus braucht dieser Einstieg keine besondere didaktische Hilfe.

Aufgabe

Als Aufgabe fassen die SuS in einem kurzen Essay zusammen, was sie über den Süden erfahren haben und wie es auf sie gewirkt hat.

While-Reading Phase

Aufgabe

Lesen des gesamten Textes mit begleitenden Aufgaben (2-3 Wochen)

Methode

Die individuelle Lektüre des gesamten restlichen Romans (Kap. 2-31) sollte spätestens mit dem Einstieg in Modul 2 in Angriff genommen werden. Alternativ kann die Lektüre in mehreren Tranchen geschehen, wobei z. B. nach Part 1 ein kurzer Test mit den Verständnisfragen (**KV 6** *Check yourself questions, Part One*) geschrieben wird.
Zur Sicherung des Leseverständnisses bieten sich vier unterschiedliche Arbeitsaufträge an:
- Schüler führen ein *Reading log* (**KV 5**) (ggf. Korrekturarbeit für den Lehrer).
- Oder sie beantworten *Check-yourself-questions* (**KV 6**).
- Oder / und sie füllen sukzessive die *Road Map* (**KV 7**) aus.

Die SuS entscheiden selbst, welche Aufgabe sie übernehmen wollen.
Die Auswertung geschieht am Anfang der *Post-Reading Phase* (siehe Modul 3).

Modul 2   Kapitel 1 als Exposition

Lernziel

Personen und Handlungsstränge kennenlernen. Motivation und Orientierung für die individuelle Lektüre gewinnen.

Aufgabe

Vorbereitendes Lesen Kapitel 1

Unterthema: Grundlagen des *Plots* im ersten Kapitel (2 Stunden)

Die Ausgangssituation der Kerngeschichte selbst ist Gegenstand eines ersten UGs, da sie nur die beiden ersten Absätze umfasst und dann erst am Ende des Buchs wieder aufgegriffen wird. Anschließend erarbeiten die Schüler im Gruppenpuzzle die übrigen Elemente selbständig.
Das erste Kapitel ist nicht nur eine Rahmenhandlung (1. Absatz), in der die Erzählperspektive der Ich-Erzählerin klar wird. Es zeigt die Ausgangssituation des Dramas, und zwar zunächst nur von der positiven Seite her. Die Kinder leben in der Kleinstadt Maycomb in mehrfacher Hinsicht geborgen und ohne Sorgen. Aufregung und Bedrohung müssen mühsam von außen in diese Welt hineingeholt werden (*The Grey Ghost; Dracula;* die Mutprobe).
Je plastischer den SuS die Grundstimmung der Ausgangssituation vertraut ist – als visuell und gefühlsmäßig Bekanntes –, desto leichter wird sich die folgende Lektüre für sie gestalten.

Methode

Das Gruppenpuzzle stellt sicher, dass jeder einzelne SuS im Unterrichtsgespräch zum Handelnden wird. Zunächst erarbeiten die SuS in Fünfergruppen (1-5) die fünf unterschiedlichen Fragestellungen (**KV 8** *Group Puzzle about chapter 1*). Ihre Einzelarbeit wird in der abschließenden Gruppenarbeit komplettiert.
Dann teilen sie sich in neue Gruppen ein (A-E) und geben als Experten ihr erarbeitetes Wissen weiter. Am Ende der Phase wissen alle SuS über alle Themen Bescheid. Die Schüler sollten ein zeitliches Limit gesetzt bekommen.

Ergebnis

Group 1 Time

- Year 1933
- Franklin D. Roosevelt has just come into office
- people talk about Great Depression
- economic situation is accepted like the weather
- people have nothing to fear but fear itself

Group 2 Where the story is set

- Alabama
- US South
- up the Creek (=Alabama River)
- off Alabama River
- in Maycomb (=Monroeville)
- feeling of a secure home

Group 3 History

- family does not date back to Battle of Hastings (1066)
- Methodist Simon Finch left Cornwall about 100 years before (1835) via Philadelphia, Jamaica, Mobile, Saint Stephens
- pious and stingy man, a little to the extreme
- established a cotton farm on Finch's Landing
- no super-farm but fairly large estate, self-sufficient
- everything was burnt down during the Civil War 4 22-24
- but they did not give up and kept their land
- they are still a family of land owners on Finch's Landing
- Atticus and Jack are the first in the family to attend University and study Law and Medicine
- feeling secure as part of the family history

Group 4 Adult members of family

- Atticus Finch, father of the children, lawyer with his own practise in Maycomb, Alabama. Widower. His wife died of a heart attack when Jean Louise was 2.
- John Hale (Jack) Finch, Atticus' brother, 10 years younger than Atticus, studied medicine in Boston, lives in Nashville, Tennessee
- Alexandra Finch, their sister, lives at Finch's Landing with her husband, a taciturn man who spends most of the time lying in his hammock and waiting for the trot-lines to be full
- Calpurnia, the black cook, almost counts as a member of the family. She looks after the Finch household and educates Scout. Atticus treats her with great respect.
- though motherless, the children grow up in sheltered family conditions

Group 5 Children

- Jean Louise (=Scout) Finch, 5, Atticus' daughter and narrator in the novel; she can read. Loves playing with Jeremy, reading stories, acting them out with Jem.
- Jeremy Atticus (=Jem) Finch, 9, Atticus son, loves playing football, working on his treehouse, reading ghost stories, acting them out with Scout, playing around the house. Tells Dill about the mysterious Boo, adds myths about Boo's eating raw squirrels and cats, going into people's gardens at night and leaving gigantic footprints.
- Charles Baker (=Dill) Harris, 6, Miss Rachel Haverford's nephew, visits during summer holidays, lives in Mississippi, parents apparently divorced, lives with his mother, is proud that he can read, a child with vivid imagination, particularly for horror stories, has seen movie Dracula, acts out book scenes with Scout and Jem, is very interested in the mysterious Boo Radley and his family, wants Boo to come out of his house where he has been for 15 years, dares Jem to touch the Radley House, funny character
- Scout, Jem and Dill develop a friendship with shared interests and abilities.

Methode

UG (das Detailwissen in ein Verständnis für die Situation überführen): Wie der Leser in die Grundstimmung, die Ausgangssituation, den Ort, die besonderen Zeitumstände der großen Depression, die Vorgeschichte der Familie Finch und die Hauptpersonen eingeführt wird. Die Geschichte bekommt sofort einen starken Sog.

Im auswertenden Schlussgespräch kann der Lehrer mit den SuS herausarbeiten, dass Scout sehr geborgen im Maycomb von 1933 lebt, beinahe wie in einem Kokon, der durch Ort und Zeit, soziale Identität (Großgrundbesitzer und Akademiker!) und historische Herkunft, durch Geschlecht und Familie definiert ist. Obwohl sie Halbwaise ist, kann ihr nichts passieren. Sie ist in jeder Hinsicht wohlbehütet.

Aufgaben

Describe Scout's situation at the outset of the story. Why does she live a sheltered life? Make references to time, place, history, the adult members of the family and the children she plays with.

Unterthema: Erste Charakterisierung der Hauptpersonen (1 Stunde)

Über die Personen Atticus, Alexandra, Jem, Dill, Scout ist in der vergangenen Stunde schon gesprochen worden. Ziel ist, diese Ergebnisse jetzt zu vertiefen. Die Schüler werden dazu in 8 Gruppen aufgeteilt und erhalten die Aufgabe, jeweils einen Steckbrief auszufüllen (**KV 9** *Characters in chapter 1*).

Ergebnis

His/her name *Alexandra's husband*
His/her age *unknown*
His/her best friends *unknown*
His/her closest relative *Alexandra*
His/her formal education *unknown*
He/she makes a living by *having a rich wife; watching his trot-lines*
He/she lives *at Finch's Landing*
His/her biggest problem/secret *never says anything*
He/she is afraid of *nothing known of*
He/she does not like to talk about *anything*

His/her name *Arthur ("Boo") Radley*
His/her age *mid-twenties or thirties*
His/her best friends *has none*
His/her closest relative *parents, brother*
His/her formal education *several years of schooling*
He/she makes a living by *unknown*
He/she lives *three doors down south of the Finches*
His/her biggest problem/secret *would have had to go to prison years ago; is now a prisoner in his own parents' house*
He/she is afraid of *coming outside? unknown*
He/she does not like to talk about *unknown*

His/her name *Atticus Finch*
His/her age *almost 50*
His/her best friends *neighbours; sheriff; all of town*
His/her closest relative *Jem and Scout; sister Alexandra and brother John Hale*
His/her formal education *home schooling; went to Law School*
He/she makes a living by *running a lawyer's practice*
He/she lives *in Maycomb*
His/her biggest problem/secret *having lost his wife*
He/she is afraid of *nothing*
He/she does not like to talk about *his neighbours; his problems*

His/her name *Calpurnia*
His/her age *unknown; around 50*
His/her best friends *not mentioned*
His/her closest relative *not mentioned*
His/her formal education *unknown*
He/she makes a living by *being Atticus's housekeeper*
He/she lives *unknown*
His/her biggest problem/secret *unknown (she is black)*
He/she is afraid of *nothing mentioned so far*
He/she does not like to talk about *her own family; her home*

His/her name *Jeremy (Jem) Atticus Finch*
His/her age *10*
His/her best friends *Dill*
His/her closest relative *Atticus, Scout, aunt Alexandra, uncle John Hale Finch*
His/her formal education *goes to school*
He/she makes a living by –
He/she lives *in Maycomb, Alabama*
His/her biggest problem/secret *loss of his mother*
He/she is afraid of *Boo Radley*
He/she does not like to talk about *his mother*

His/her name *Miss Stephanie Crawford*
His/her age *around 50*
His/her best friends *none known*
His/her closest relative *unknown*
His/her formal education *unknown*
He/she makes a living by *unknown*
He/she lives *two houses down south of the Finches*
His/her biggest problem/secret *perhaps loneliness*
He/she is afraid of *nothing known*
He/she does not like to talk about – *on the contrary. She gossips about everything and everybody.*

His/her name *Mr Radley*
His/her age *about 70*
His/her best friends *unknown, unfriendly person*
His/her closest relative *wife and two sons, Nathan and Arthur (Boo)*
His/her formal education *unknown*
He/she makes a living by *unknown*
He/she lives *three houses down south of the Finches*
His/her biggest problem/secret *what happened to Boo*
He/she is afraid of *nothing known*
He/she does not like to talk about *anything*

> His/her name **Jean Louise (Scout) Finch**
> His/her age **6**
> His/her best friends **brother Jem and Dill**
> His/her closest relative **Atticus, Jem, aunt Alexandra, uncle John Hale Finch**
> His/her formal education **none so far**
> He/she makes a living by **–**
> He/she lives **in Maycomb, Alabama**
> His/her biggest problem/secret **what Boo Radley is like**
> He/she is afraid of **Boo**
> He/she does not like to talk about **her late mother**

Methode

Im anschließenden UG herausarbeiten, dass die Menschen bei aller Gegensätzlichkeit konfliktfrei miteinander leben (weiß-schwarz; straffällig-nicht straffällig; arm-reich; geschwätzig-diskret; Familie mit beiden Elternteilen – Familie ohne Mutter). In der Exposition ist die Welt noch in Ordnung, obgleich fast jeder ein kleines Geheimnis hütet. Aber die Welt trägt bereits Konfliktpotenzial in sich.

Fragestellung

How do all these people get on with each other?

Methode

Schlussabstimmung mit der Klasse: eine Glaubwürdigkeitsskala mit Werten von 1 bis 10 erstellen. Dazu Tafelbild als Zeichnung.

Fragestellung

On a scale of trustworthiness running from one to ten, ten being the best, how would you rate …?

Aufgabe

Give a short characterization of one of the main characters.

Unterthema: Stilmittel analysieren und erklären (2 Stunden)

Da im ersten Kapitel bereits alle Stilmittel voll entwickelt sind, lohnt es sich, den Blick dafür zu schärfen.

Methode

Die doppelte Perspektive sollte im UG gemeinsam erarbeitet werden: es ist einmal die Perspektive der erwachsenen Scout, die Rückschau auf die Kindheitsereignisse hält, und dann die Perspektive des Kindes, das vieles nicht begreift. Komik entsteht dadurch, dass das Unbegriffene stehengelassen wird und der Leser mehr weiß als das Kind.

Fragestellung

What do you think is the age of the narrator of the story?

Methode

Drei weitere Stilmittel sollen in getrennten Arbeitsaufträgen zunächst in Einzelarbeit erarbeitet werden. (**KV 10** *Analysing literary means in chapter 1*) Dazu sollte die Vorgehensweise bei den jeweiligen Stilmitteln kurz erklärt werden:

Humour
Watch out for small observations in descriptions and dialogue. The book is full of humour. You will detect different kinds of humour – there is a lot of understatement, exaggeration, euphemism, irony and sarcasm, as well as all sorts of unusual observations, perceptions and fantasies from a child's perspective.

Irritations
This is not a literary category but it helps to understand the gloomy character of the first chapter. Look out for allusions to death, blood or other scary details.

Subplots
These are stories that are not vitally important for the main story. Which ones can you identify? And why may they be there?

Die o. g. verschiedenen Typen von Humor sollten ggf. an der Tafel festgehalten werden. Da die SuS für diese Aufgabe das gesamte erste Kapitel noch einmal durchsuchen müssen, sollten sie ca. 45 Minuten zur Bewältigung ihrer Aufgabe bekommen. Anschließend sollten SuS, die das gleiche Thema bearbeitet haben, zu zweit oder zu dritt ihre Ergebnisse austauschen, diskutieren und ergänzen.

Kommentar

Das Buch ist von einem Humor durchtränkt, der zum Teil aus der Kinderperspektive und zum Teil aus einer Allmachtsperspektive kommt – ich finde zum Beispiel auch das Bild des Onkels sehr komisch, der, nachdem er die reiche Tante Alexandra geheiratet hat, nur noch in der Hängematte liegt und auf fiese Art mit Legeangeln fischt. Mehr muss man über diesen Mann gar nicht wissen. Ein Großteil des Humors kommt verdeckt daher. Man muss die Bilder schon sehr genau vor Augen haben, um die Komik darin zu entdecken. – *Subplots:* auf einiges, wie etwa den Subplot von Atticus's ersten Klienten, die anschließend gehängt wurden, könnte man im Sinne einer stringenten Erzählung verzichten. Es ist aber auch im Sinne eines *foreshadowing* zu verstehen – dasselbe Schicksal wird später Tom Robinson ereilen. Auch die Cunninghams, diese wandelnden Metaphern schlechter Gesellschaft, müssten eigentlich nicht so ausführlich beschrieben werden, wäre da nicht später die Szene mit dem Mob,

Modul 2

der Atticus und Tom lynchen will. Dort steht wieder ein Cunningham in vorderster Linie. Auch hier also *foreshadowing*. Und ein *private joke* ist auch noch eingebaut: Der Mädchenname von Harper Lees Mutter lautete *Cunningham Finch*.

Ergebnis

Insbesondere im Bereich Humor sollte man den SuS auch die Möglichkeit lassen aufzuführen, was sie persönlich lustig finden, selbst wenn sie die Art des Humors nicht kategorisieren können. Dies kann später gut im UG geklärt werden. Für das Thema Humor ist unten also nur eine kleine mögliche Auswahl an Ergebnissen gegeben.

Task 1

Humour

- 5 6 dispatched → = killed → euphemism/understatement
- 5 13 be present at their departure → = death → euphemism/sarkasmus
- 5 25 because of Simon Finch's industry Atticus was related by blood or marriage to nearly every family in the town → industry → irony
- 6 6 a time of vague optimism for some of the people. Maycomb County had recently been told that it had nothing to fear but fear itself. → irony
- 7 2 Radley place was inhabited by an unknown entity → not deserving the title *man* → childlike misconception/exaggeration
- 7 4 Mrs Dubose was plain hell. → exaggeration
- 7 15 I'm Ch. Baker Harris. I can read. → childlike naivety
- 7 25 I'm little but I'm old. → child's perspective
- 9 39 Radley pecans would kill you → childlike naivety
- 11 25 received the best secondary education to be had in the state → irony
- 12 28 kept him chained to the bed → child's perception/fantasy
- 14 14ff. Jem's "reasonable" description of Boo → irony → child's perception/fantasy/exaggeration

Task 2

Irritations

- 6 28 our mother died from a sudden heart attack → death as fate
- 7 2 an unknown entity → scary
- 8 23 Dill's father: "Is he dead?" → death as a natural aspect of life
- 9 20 malevolent phantom → scary
- 9 21-38 People said … → scary
- 9 39 Radley pecans would kill you → death as an imminent danger
- 12 2-7 Scissors episode → scary
- 12 8 Arthur was killing them all → death as an imminent danger
- 12 28 kept him chained to the bed most of the time → scary
- 13 14 Mr Radley was dying → death as fate
- 14 15 he dined on raw squirrels → scary
- 15 28 strike a match under him → cruel

Task 3

Subplots

- 4 28–32 Aunt Alexandra and her lazy husband → slight decadence has reached the family tree
- 4 38–5 15 Atticus' first two clients were hanged → a failed defence with a cruel result
- 5 27–6 8 a short history of Maycomb, a tired and slow town at the time → presentation of a remote provincial place that doesn't appear to be threatening
- 6 23–29 Scout's mother's life and death → death plays a minor role in Scout's life
- 7 36–8 24 Dill's story → another one-parent child like Jem and Scout
- 10 1–15 The Radley's story → a strange family, keeping to themselves and making themselves outsiders in the world of white Maycomb
- 10 36–11 29 Boo's story → a rather harmless and comical episode
- 12 2-7 Boo's scissors episode → is this just neighbourhood legend or is there some truth to it?

Methode

Die Auswertung der Arbeitsergebnisse sollte in einem UG münden, in dem zusammenfassend die Wirkung des 1. Kapitels auf die SuS besprochen wird.

Fragestellung

What do you know about the place and its people after reading the first chapter?

> **Ergebnis**
> The reader becomes familiar with
> - the location and its history,
> - a number of characters, their individual stories and attitudes,
> - the children's carefree life and their little fears.

Aufgaben

Describe how in the exposition of the book, behind the picture of a whole and good world, the potential of a horrible story is lurking. Refer to allusions of horror which at this stage come in from the outside world.

Post-Reading Phase

Modul 3 Die Themen des Romans (2-3 Stunden)

Lernziel

Hauptthemen des Romans auf der Basis der Leseaufträge isolieren.

Methode

Damit die Interpretationsarbeit am Roman funktionieren kann, müssen alle SuS unbedingt das Buch in voller Länge gelesen haben.

Als Einstieg soll hier noch einmal dem Prinzip der Visualisierung gefolgt werden, indem SuS, die diesen Leseauftrag bearbeitet haben, die Topographie des Romans anhand der *Road Map* präsentieren.

Dass Harper Lee den fiktiven Ort Maycomb nach ihrer Heimatstadt Monroeville gestaltet hat, ist kein Geheimnis. Als zusätzliche Aufgabe können die SuS sich aus dem Internet Photos aus dem heutigen Monroeville und dem „Maycomb" der 30er Jahre herunterladen. Die Häuser von Boo, Scout und das Courthouse sind als Abbildungen im www zu finden. Sie geben auch eine hübsche Ergänzung für ein eventuell einzurichtendes Portfolio ab.

> **Ergebnis**
> siehe **KV 7.2**

Methode

Es ist nicht sinnvoll, die vielen Detailfragen des *Reading Logs* und der *Check Yourself Questions* im Unterricht zu besprechen. Es empfiehlt sich hingegen für den L im UG diejenigen Kapitel (*Reading Log*) und die Details zum Verständnis dieser Kapitel (*Check Yourself Questions*) anzusprechen, die im Roman besonderes Gewicht haben. Dabei liegt natürlich nahe, zunächst auf die im 1. Kapitel erwähnten Personen und angelegten Handlungsstränge zurückzugreifen und sie den SuS in Erinnerung zu rufen.

Es bleibt jedem L überlassen, entweder die Leseaufträge zwecks Kontrolle einzusammeln oder aber durch Verteilen der Musterlösungen (**KVs 5.2, 6.3, 6.4**) zum Schluss der Stunde einen Mindestkenntnisstand sicherzustellen.

Fragestellung

Which topics introduced in chapter 1 remain important for the whole novel?

> **Ergebnis**
> - Life in Maycomb
> - The children's friendship
> - The children and Boo Radley
> - Humour
> - Scary events

Fragestellung

What is 'To Kill a Mockingbird' about?

Ergebnis
- Racial segregation
- Growing up and learning the lessons of life ('Bildungsroman')
- Losing one's innocence
- Injustice in court and a man's fight against it
- Atticus – a model father and lawyer
- Becoming a woman and thus being reduced to a "lower caste"
- The coexistence of Good and Evil (most people are nice when you finally see them)
- Small-town life
- Modern Gothic novel (unnatural snow fall; fire in Miss Maudie's house; superstitions about Boo; mad dog; Halloween party; Dracula, *The Grey Ghost* and other horror stories)

Ein Tafelanschrieb in Form einer *Mind Map* erleichtert es, zusammenhängende Themen und Unterthemen mit aufzunehmen:

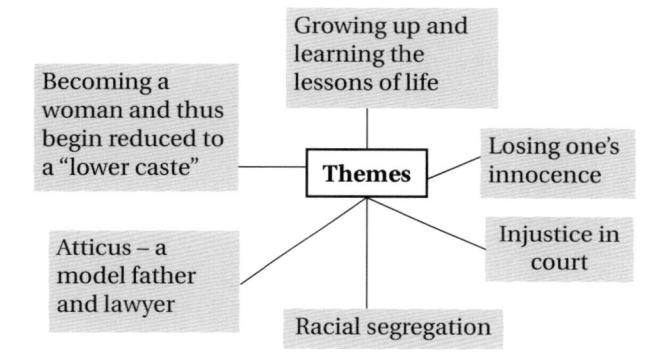

```
                Growing up and
                learning the
                lessons of life
Becoming a
woman and thus
begin reduced to                    Losing one's
a "lower caste"    ── Themes ──     innocence

    Atticus – a                     Injustice in
    model father                    court
    and lawyer
                Racial segregation
```

Aufgabe

Als Aufgabe können die Schüler die *Mind Map* ggfs. ergänzen und entsprechende Sätze zum Thema *The great themes of 'To Kill a Mockingbird'* formulieren.

Modul 4   Lessons of life – climbing into people's skins (8–10 Stunden)

Methode

In diesen Unterrichtsstunden sollen die SuS ein wenig von dem nachvollziehen, was Scout als Lernprozess miterlebt hat. Sie benutzen zunächst ihre *Reading Logs* (**KV 5**) noch einmal, um die einzelnen Lebenslektionen zu erfahren. – In der nächsten Stunde zeichnen sie nach, wie Scout nach und nach begreift, in welcher Lebenssituation sich Tom Robinson eigentlich befindet. – Um die Situation mit dem Mobauflauf wirklich zu begreifen, wird anhand des Liedes *Strange Fruit* eine Stunde über die Geschichte der Lynchjustiz in den Südstaaten diskutiert. – Erst danach erschließt sich die volle Spannung der Mob-Szene, die nun analysiert werden kann, sowohl von ihrem massenpsychologischen Standpunkt aus, als auch schlicht daraus, dass Scout die Empfehlung ihres Vaters umsetzt, die Menschen aus ihrer eigenen Haut heraus zu begreifen. – Auch Scouts Begreifen von Boo Radleys Situation vollzieht sich in Stufen, die noch einmal nachgezeichnet werden. – Während der Gerichtsverhandlung fällt es Scout besonders leicht, sich in die Rolle des Staatsanwalts hineinzuversetzen – während Dill die lebensbedrohliche Situation von Tom Robinson nahezu mitlebt. – Optional ist die humorvolle Situation, einer Klatschtante wie Stephanie Crawford die Stirn zu bieten: auch sie versetzt sich schließlich in die Haut anderer Menschen, jedoch nur, um sich selbst als Informantin interessant zu machen.

Unterthema: 31 Kapitel als Lebenslektionen für Scout (2–3 Stunden)

Lernziel

Erkennen der Grundstruktur(en) des Romans.

Methode

Machen Sie die SuS darauf aufmerksam, dass Scout in jedem Kapitel etwas lernt. *To Kill a Mockingbird* ist auch ein *Bildungsroman*, wobei Bildung als Herzensbildung, als Charakterausformung verstanden wird. Das Wort *Bildungsroman* ist auch ein Fremdwort im Englischen.

Fragestellung

What is the rationale behind dividing the book into 31 chapters?

Ergebnis

Each chapter
- contains a kind of episode,
- a statement that gives a new explanation of something,
- a new understanding of a fact or situation for Scout.

Methode

Im nächsten Schritt soll in GA überblickartig dargestellt werden, wie Scout in jedem Kapitel eine „Lektion lernt". Die Frage nach den Lernabschnitten ist keine Inhaltsfrage, sondern eine Strukturfrage – ein Strukturmerkmal des Romans wird darin erkannt, ein formales Mittel.

Die SuS sollten dazu ihre *Reading Logs* (**KV 5**) zu Hilfe nehmen. Jede Gruppe analysiert jeweils etwa 5 Kapitel und erstellt dann gemeinsam eine Wandzeitung. Anschließend wird die große Wandzeitung gemeinsam gelesen und im UG bewertet und diskutiert.

Fragestellung

What does Scout learn in each chapter?

Ergebnis

She learns …
1. … a lot of myths about Boo Radley.
2. … that it is disadvantageous to come to school already knowing what it is all about (knowing how to read).
3. … that putting herself into other people's skins helps to understand their curious ways.
4. … that there may be a person with a laugh and a soul inhabiting the Radley house after all.
5. … from Miss Maudie that Boo can be seen as a human being who deserves sympathy.
6. … that getting too close to a forbidden sphere can put your life in danger.
7. … by filling a hole in a perfectly healthy tree, Nathan Radley stops a mysterious communication.
8. … that Boo really must be a gentle, caring person who slipped the blanket over her shoulders without her noticing.
9. … that losing her temper in the face of unjust accusations is bad but hard not to do.
10. … that her father is a brilliant marksman, but people like him never take pride in their talents.
11. … that the nasty old lady from nextdoor was in fact a couragous woman who fought her morphine addiction.
12. … to see the black congregation as a well-organised community in its own right and that Calpurnia leads a "double life" in two societies.
13. … that her time as a tomboy might be coming to an end.
14. … that her brother takes on Atticus' airs by betraying her secret that Dill has escaped from home.
15. … that by disobeying a rule – Jem wants to look after Atticus who in turn looks after Tom Robinson – the children did something right.
16. … that Miss Maudie despises a crowd that indulges in other people's misfortune.
17. … that evidence alone will not necessarily help to achieve justice.
18. … to recognize an obvious liar: Tom could never have strangled Mayella the way she claims.
19. … that it makes Dill sick when he sees how the prosecutor treats Tom.
20. … that the alcoholic Dolphus Raymond can be an accepted member of society, the *nigger lover* Raymond can not.
21. … that Atticus gives them permission to come back for the jury's verdict: growing up means taking part in the adult life.
22. … people react differently to defeat of justice.
23. … about the effect of her own communication with Walter Cunningham during the mob scene: the only member of the jury who wanted to find Tom Robinson innocent was a Cunningham.
24. … about bigotry: the racist ladies enjoy listening to the missionary who tries to reform Africans. – She also learns about carrying on with one's life's chores no matter what happened.
25. … that Tom Robinson must have given up on white justice and that Jem takes the subject of death very much to heart.
26. … about double talk or bigotry on national level. While Hitler's killing the innocent Jews makes his administration a dictatorship, America retains the status of a democracy even though it is killing innocent Blacks.
27. … that although Tom is dead, the case isn't settled for Bob Ewell.
28. … how it feels to be the victim of an intended murder.
29. … that the mysterious *Grey Ghost* of her childhood has saved her life.
30. … that Atticus finally gives in when the sheriff bends the law to spare Boo the torment of a public appearance in court.
31. … that she has grown up. Her childhood fantasy about luring Boo Radley out of his house has been fulfilled. He is a real person, entertained by her on her own porch. He is more timid than she is. He needs her. She fulfills his wish in reply to the only sentence he utters: "Will you take me home?"

Methode

Falls noch Zeit ist, könnte hier besprochen, welche anderen Elemente dem Roman eine Struktur oder roten Faden geben.

Fragestellung

Are there other themes or topics – apart from the 31 chapters with their lessons for Scout – that run through the novel and give it structure?

Modul 4

Ergebnis
- time / especially seasons
- Dill's visits
- the trial (approx. ¼ of the whole novel)
- the neighbourhood and their attitudes

Unterthema: Scout gewinnt Verständnis für Toms Lebenssituation (1 Stunde)

Lernziel

Erkennen, inwiefern sich Scouts Haltung zu Tom im Laufe des Romans verändert.

Methode

Scout begreift erst ganz allmählich, wer dieser Tom Robinson ist, welches Schicksal ihm droht und was das für seine Familie und die schwarze *community* bedeutet. Die Tatsache der Vergewaltigung begreift sie überhaupt nie, was sie aber nicht stört. Sie akzeptiert sehr vergnügt Atticus' juristische Definition und kann nicht begreifen, weshalb sich Calpurnia wegen einer solchen Petitesse so aufregt.
Diesen Prozess des Begreifens nachzuvollziehen ist Gegenstand dieser Stunde. Dazu teilt sich die Klasse in sieben Gruppen auf. Jede Gruppe erhält die Aufgabe, eines der Stadien herauszuarbeiten, in denen Scout Verständnis für Tom gewinnt (**KV 11**). Aus jeder Gruppe präsentieren ein oder zwei SuS die Ergebnisse.

Fragestellung

How does Scout perceive Tom's situation?

Ergebnisse

Gruppe 1
before: she is ignorant about the implications of the notion *nigger*
after: still has only a vague idea about Tom's trial, but since Atticus is involved, it must be a good cause

Group 2
before: she is mad at Francis in an unspecified matter
after: understands that Atticus does not just fight *a case* but injustice (does not understand in which precise form)

Group 3
before: she has never thought about there being a whole black community and Calpurnia belonging to it
after: witnessing the reaction of the congregation she knows that Helen's situation is terrible

Group 4
before: she has a vague sense of Atticus and Tom being in danger
after: still isn't aware of the danger her family is in along with Tom Robinson

Group 5
before: the children treat it as a kind of dare to go to the courthouse, disobeying Atticus
after: they realize how the two different worlds are put into two different spaces – naively, they mix up this order by sitting with the blacks

Group 6
before: the children know that Atticus has a difficult case
after: first they think that by fighting fair and with the better arguments Atticus has saved the innocent Tom – after the verdict, Jem cries with disappointment, but they still do not think Tom will have to die.

Group 7
before: she knows that democracy means equal rights and no special priviliges
after: realizes that democracy might not apply to blacks, because the same people who hate Hitler for his persecution of the Jews treat black people badly (double standards)

→ Tom's case leads to a deeper understanding of the social and political situation of the black people in the US in general.

Unterthema: Lynchmord – Billie Holidays Lied *Strange Fruit* und seine Folgen (2 Stunden)

Lernziel

Das Lied *Strange Fruit* im historischen Kontext der Lynchjustiz verstehen.

Methode

Unbegriffen bleiben wohl bis zum Schluss bei Scout die Implikationen von Vergewaltigung und der häufig unter diesem Vorwand geübten Lynchjustiz gegenüber Farbigen. Wie die Realität der Lynchjustiz aussah, ist Gegenstand dieser Stunde. Als Einstieg können die SuS ihr Vorwissen aktivieren oder spekulieren, wie die Mob-Szene in Kapitel 15 hätte anders verlaufen können.

Fragestellung

Can you imagine what would have happened if Scout hadn't saved the situation in the mob scene in chapter 15?

Methode

Billie Holidays Lied *Strange Fruit*, das drastisch aber dezent poetisch einen in einer Pappel erhängten Schwarzen beschreibt, ist ein Meilenstein in der Bürgerrechtsbewegung in den USA. Die Worte des Liedes, der Vortrag durch Billie Holiday und seine Wirkung sind Erkenntnisgegenstand dieser Stunde.
Zu diesem Thema ist bei Klett unter der Nummer 3-12-532358-2 eine preiswerte Dokumentation erhältlich.

Nachdem die Klasse gemeinsam das Gedicht gelesen hat (**KV 12.1, 12.2**) und Verständnisfragen geklärt sind, sehen sie zusammen die Dokumentation oder alternativ nur ein Video an (z. B.: http://www.youtube.com/watch?v=h4ZyuULy9zs), auf dem Billie Holiday das Lied singt. Dann werden in GA unterschiedliche Aufgaben erarbeitet:

Gruppe 1: Vergleich des Gedichts mit dem zugrundeliegenden Foto.
Gruppe 2: Übertragung in poetisches Deutsch.
Gruppe 3: Darstellung der dichterischen Mittel.
Gruppe 4: Kurzer Vortrag zur Geschichte des Liedes.
Gruppe 5: Kurzer Vortrag zur Geschichte der Lynchjustiz in den USA.

Falls in der Stunde kein Internet zur Verfügung steht, sollten die beiden letzten Gruppen den jeweiligen Ausdruck zur Verfügung haben. Für Gruppe 5 wären Ausdrucke der Fälle von 1921-1940, die auch die Ermordung von Thomas Shipp und Abram Smith enthalten, sinnvoll.

Ergebnis (Gruppe 3)

- 3 verses
- rhymes AABB throughout
- hard male end rhyme: only seemingly a light-footed rhythm
- images: blood on the leaves, blood at the root, body swinging in the breeze, bulging eyes, twisted mouth, burning flesh, fruit for crows to pluck, rain to gather, wind to suck, sun to rot, tree to drop → poem/song is loaded with oppressive images
- metaphors: fruit, crop
- predominant monosyllabics: heavy, meaningful sound
- contrasts: fruit → blood; pastoral and gallant → bulging eyes and twisted mouth; magnolia sweet and fresh → burning flesh

Methode

In einer Abschlussdiskussion beschreiben die Schüler, wie der Anblick des Photos aus **KV 12,1**, nach dem das Lied gedichtet wurde, auf sie selbst gewirkt hat.

Fragestellung

What shocks you more, the photo or the poem/song?

Aufgaben

Write a poem of your own about the photograph.
or
Summarize the effect of Billie Holiday's song *Strange Fruit* on American Society.

Methode

Die Beschäftigung mit *Strange Fruit* könnte man natürlich sehr weit ausdehnen. Allein die Gedichtinterpretation könnte mindestens zwei Stunden umfassen. Die Gruppenreferate zu den fünf Einzelprojekten könnten mindestens eine Stunde in Anspruch nehmen. Eine Diskussion zum gerade wieder auflebenden Interesse an Billie Holiday würde sich anbieten, da mit der Präsidentschaft Obamas Billie Holidays Anklage zu einem unerwarteten und positiven Ende gekommen ist. Diese Stundenskizze ist daher nur als Anregung mit den wichtigsten Quellen aufzufassen.

Eingebettet in den Arbeitszusammenhang von *To Kill a Mockingbird* erfüllt es die Funktion zu zeigen, wie schnell man mit dem Strick bei der Hand war, und sei es nur, um „ein Exempel zu statuieren, damit die Schwarzen nicht zu frech werden", – genau wie Miss Gates in Kapitel 26 sagt.

Zynisch ausgedrückt, sollen die Schüler in dieser Stunde eine Lehrstunde zum „Alltag des Lynchens" erhalten. Festhalten sollte jeder, dass es sich um eine illegale Tötung ohne Gerichtsverhandlung, also um Mord handelt.

Unterthema: Die Mob-Szene als Lehrstunde (2 Stunden)

Lernziel

Wichtige Aspekte von Massenverhalten in der Mob-Szene erkennen.

Methode

Erst vor dem Hintergrund der brutalen Realität des Lynchens wird restlos klar, was in der Mob-Szene wirklich auf dem Spiel steht: nichts Geringeres als das Leben von Tom Robinson, und die Unversehrtheit von Atticus und den drei Kindern. Dass es Scout gelingt, diese lebensbedrohliche Situation massenpsychologisch herumzureißen, ist letztlich das Ergebnis von Atticus' Empfehlung, sich in die Haut der anderen zu versetzen. Wenngleich Scout das hier naiv und eher zufällig umsetzt, so rettet sie damit – gerade wegen ihrer Naivität – Tom das Leben.

Aufgabe der SuS ist es in dieser Stunde, die Stufen zu identifizieren, in denen die Macht der Masse zunächst ansteigt und dann depotenziert wird. Atticus und die Kinder werden vom Objekt zum Subjekt der Situation. In wie vielen Stufen die Eskalation und Deeskalation gesehen wird, ist eine Frage der Sichtweise. Deshalb empfiehlt es sich, die Ausgangsfrage in GA zu lösen und die Ergebnisse entweder einzeln präsentieren zu lassen oder im UG zu besprechen. Der L kann die Ergebnisse gut in einer Kurve bzw. einem *cline*, festhalten, um so den Grad der Eskalation oder Deeskalation

Modul 4

zu veranschaulichen. Alternativ kann er die Arbeitsgruppen auch dazu auffordern, selbst eine anschauliche Darstellungsweise für ihre Ergebnisse zu finden.

Fragestellung

What are the factors that prevented the mob from getting out of hand in the scene in front of the jail?

Auswertung

166 35 deescalation: '… don't wake him up.' → ignoring the mob's motives
167 8 escalation: '… didn't you think a'that, Mr Finch?' → misjudgement on Atticus part, statement of mob to plan something unlawful
168 14 escalation: … and grabbed Jem roughly … → mob doesn't want children to watch their violence, but first physical aggression is against a child
168 16-23 escalation: … see him fall back … 'You got 15 seconds …' → shamed by a little girl they still give Atticus a menacing ultimatum
168 27 escalation: 'Please Jem, take them home.' → Atticus hasn't even got power over his own children
168 30 ff escalation: … buttoned up … cold-natured … sullen-looking → Scout becomes aware of the danger of the anonymous crowd
169 1 deescalation: 'Hey Mr Cunningham.' → crowd is no longer anonymous
169 9 f deescalation: …uncomfortable … looked away … → showing guilt and insecurity
169 15-27 deescalation: 'Don't you remember me, …?' … '… Tell him hey for me, won't you?' → talking friendly and with sympathy, puts herself into his skin. Topics: entailment, paying her father, his son → he's got problems, he's poor, he's a father → he's a human being
170 4 ff deescalation '…not to worry … you all'd ride it out together' → friendship, mutual interest, Atticus' ability to help Cunningham

Methode

Zur Bewertung der Szene könnten die SuS abschließend diskutieren, inwiefern sie realistisch ist und somit allgemeinere Gültigkeit haben könnte.

Fragestellung

Is the effect that Scout's words have on Cunningham realistic?

Unterthema: Scout gewinnt Verständnis für Boo Radley (2 Stunden)

Methode

Es ist vielleicht Scouts größtes Erlebnis am Ende des Romangeschehens, dass sie den echten Boo kennenlernt. Die Figur Boo Radley steht so am Anfang und am Ende des Romans und bildet die Klammer um die Kindheitserlebnisse von Jem, Scout und Dill. Scouts sich verändernde Wahrnehmung und ihr Heranwachsen lassen sich hieran – ähnlich wie in ihrer Wahrnehmung Tom Robinsons – demonstrieren. Bei begrenzter Zeit könnte also auf dieses Unterthema verzichtet werden, bzw. es könnte den SuS zur selbstständigen Bearbeitung als Aufgabe gestellt werden.

Lernziel

Erkennen, dass die ‚Menschwerdung' Boos eine Metapher für das Heranwachsen Scouts ist.

Methode

Drei verschiedene Aktivitäten bieten sich an. Sie können von drei verschiedenen Gruppen gleichzeitig oder von allen nacheinander bearbeitet werden:
(1) Rückschau auf die Stationen der Bekanntschaft.
(2) Deren pantomimische Darstellung.
Die Schüler sollen hier nicht nur ihre kinaesthetische Intelligenz einbringen dürfen, sondern sollen diesmal ihrerseits als Pantomimen in die Haut der Romanfiguren schlüpfen. Die SuS können dabei entweder unabhängig von (1) wenige Schlüsselszenen heraussuchen, proben und vorführen. Oder nach Beantwortung von (1) können die Szenen unter die ganze Lerngruppe aufgeteilt werden.
(3) Analyse des Schlusskapitels.

Fragestellungen (1)

What do you think are the important stages in the children's encounters with Boo Radley?
How do they influence Scout's view of Boo Radley?

Ergebnis

- a scary monster that no-one has ever seen (p. 12, p. 14), the dare (p. 16) → fear and overcoming fear
- children trying to climb into the Radleys' skins by acting out scenes (p. 43, p. 55) → fascination
- mended trousers and knot-hole episodes (pp. 65 ff.): Jem starts suspecting that Boo might be behind those friendly gestures → reconsidering Boo's character
- Boo covers Scout's shoulders during the fire, Jem fully realizes that Boo has been kind to them and defends him (p. 79 f.). → good to them and maybe harmless

- Scout learns from Jem that Boo might want to stay in the house because people have treated him badly in the past. → vulnerable and shy human being
- Boo saves the children's lives by killing Ewell (p. 289 ff.). When Scout recognizes him (p. 298) she is overwhelmed by emotion. → Boo as their protector and shy friend
- Boo sits beside Scout, Scout leads him to Jem and takes him home (p. 305 f.). → Scout helps and protects Boo
- Standing on Boo's porch Scout sees everything from Boo's angle. → she finally understands him by 'standing in his shoes'

Fragestellung (2)

Which developments become visible in the pantomime?

Fragestellungen (3)

How does Scout see Boo in the last chapter?
What does the new perception say about her?

Ergebnis

- uncertain movements, physically weak or exhausted
- timid, quiet, doesn't speak
- needing help and encouragement (**306** 11 ff.)
- asking for help (**306** 18) 'like a child afraid of the dark'
- gentle (**306** 12, 36)
- → Scout perceives Arthur as the person he really is and understands that he needs her help and support in this situation. In her new role she shows that she is growing up.

Unterthema: Scout versteht den Staatsanwalt (1 Stunde)

Lernziel

Verstehen, wie Scout und Dill das Kreuzverhör unterschiedlich wahrnehmen.

Methode

In dieser Stunde lösen die SuS zwei Sichten des Kreuzverhörs argumentativ aus dem Text (**216** 27–**220** 20) heraus. Dill sagt, Gilmore war unfair, Scout sagt, er war fair. Dill sieht die Situation aus der Sicht von Tom, Scout aus der Sicht der Daseinsberechtigung von Juristen.
Diese Gegenüberstellung zweier Sichten fechten die SuS argumentativ in einem ‚Kugellager' aus.
Kopiervorlage **KV 13**: der linke S in einer Bank erhält jeweils die Aufgabe A, der rechte die Aufgabe B.
Die SuS lesen **216** 27–**220** 20 und machen sich aus der Sicht von Dill (Gruppe A) bzw. Scout (Gruppe B) Notizen zum Verlauf des Kreuzverhörs. Zeitvorgabe: 20-25 Minuten.
Zum ‚Kugellager' formen die SuS zwei konzentrische Kreise: Die eine Gruppe innen, die andere außen. Die SuS diskutieren anschließend jeweils aus der Sicht von Dill bzw. Scout das Kreuzverhör. Nach ca. 5 Minuten geht der innere Kreis 2 Personen weiter nach links, nach weiteren 5 Minuten bewegt sich der äußere Kreis 2 Personen nach links weiter. Durch das Weiterbewegen sollen die SuS neue Argumente kennen lernen und selbst entwickeln.
Die SuS lernen auf diese Weise, selbst erarbeitete Argumente gegenüber unterschiedlichen Partnern vorzutragen und strikt eine bestimmte Sichtweise beizubehalten, auch wenn die nicht unbedingt ihrer eigenen Meinung entspricht.
Lehrerverhalten während der Diskussion: Mit Clipboard von einem zum anderen gehen und gute Argumente mitschreiben, anschließend noch einmal lobend hervorheben.
Einige Argumente, die die SuS finden könnten:

Ergebnisse

Dill:

- **216** 28 addressing Tom as "Robinson" instead of "Mr Robinson" → degrading
- **216** 30 "What did the nigger look like …" → trying to make Tom look violent
- **216** 32 Even though Tom was attacked he was convicted → trying to make him look partly guilty
- **217** 14 addressing Tom as "boy" → degrading
- **217** 15 "Had your eye on her …" → assumption, insinuation
- **217** 6-7 "Good at busting up chifferobes …"; 9-10 "strong enough to choke the breath out of a woman"; 16-17 "mighty polite" → further insinuations
- **217** 32 "… from sheer goodness"; 35 "… mighty good fellow …", 36 Mr Gilmer smiled grimly → irony used to undermine Tom's credibility
- **218** 1 "*You* felt sorry for *her*, …" → Gilmore expresses that as a negro Tom is not allowed to feel sorry for his white superiors: an insult of white people in the eyes of the jury
- **218** 32 "If you had a clear conscience …" → insinuating Tom was frightened because he did not have a clean conscience
- **219** 4 "Are you being impudent …" → trying to undermine belief in Tom's credibility and friendliness
- **219** 35 "… Mr Finch didn't act that way to Mayella …" → you don't just treat your own witnesses well

Modul 4

Scout:
- 219 15 "Ain't you feeling good?" → Scout is not aware why Dill is upset, because she accepts Mr Gilmer's way of interrogating Tom
- 219 26f "… talking so hateful to him –" – "Dill, that's his job. …" → Mr Gilmer is only doing his job as a prosecutor
- 219 30ff "… It was the way he said it …" – "He's supposed to act that way …" → Mr Gilmer is behaving according to the rules
- 219 34 "… those were his own witnesses." → he doesn't treat them better than Tom because they are white
- 220 1 "… after all he's just a Negro." → Mr Gilmer addresses Tom in the normal and appropriate way and there is no ill will on his part
- 220 5 "That's just Mr Gilmer's way. …" → his way of talking is part of his personal interrogation strategy
- 220 7 "… like he wasn't half trying. …" → he wasn't as hard on Tom as he usually is on others

Fakultative Zusatzstunde:
Der Klatschtante die Stirn bieten (2 Stunden)

Lernziel
Sich höflich und bestimmt gegenüber Klatschmäulern verhalten.

Methode
Dieses Zusatzmodul übt in spielerischer Form sprachliches Verhalten gegenüber Klatschmäulern. Die SuS üben dabei in Form eines stummen Schreibgesprächs, der allzu einfühlsamen Stephanie Crawford Paroli zu bieten.
Der L hat ca. 10 DIN-A3-Bögen auf einer langen Reihe von Tischen ausgebreitet. Daneben liegen mitteldicke Filzstifte.
Der L erklärt das Konzept eines stummen Schreibgesprächs. Alternativ kann L die Arbeitsanweisungen auch ausgedruckt als OHP-Folien oder Tafelanschrieb eingeben. Dann ist der Dialog absolut schweigend.
Der L befragt die SuS, was sie über Stephanie Crawford wissen. Die Antworten werden nur schriftlich gegeben.

Ergebnis
- neighbourhood scold
- gossipmonger
- told scissors story
- does not let the Radleys keep to themselves as Atticus does

Methode
L befragt SuS, was die Kinder im 1. Kapitel von S. Crawford über Boo Radley erfahren. Die Antworten werden wieder nur schriftlich gegeben.
Auf den ersten DIN-A-3-Bogen schreibt L mit Filzstift *Boo*, auf den nächsten *The Radley family*.
Die SuS schreiben auf, was sie an Informationen und Klatsch über die Radleys erinnern. Hinter jedem Satz lassen sie Raum für einen Kommentar.

Ergebnis

Boo …
- … is a maniac and he's dangerous.
- … eats raw squirrels and cats.
- … locked the Maycomb County beadle in the outhouse one night, together with the wrong crowd. After that, his father had him locked up in his own house.
- … comes out at night only and peeps into Miss Stephanie's window.
- … leaves his footprints in gardens.

The Radley family
- … never talk to the neighbours.
- … don't go to church on Sundays.
- Mr Radley goes to town at 11.30h every day.
- He never greets anyone.
- He only coughs in response to a greeting.

Methode
Der L beschriftet weitere Bögen mit den Namen Miss Maudie, Dill Harris, Bob Ewell, Tom Robinson, Atticus, Scout, Mayella.
Die SuS gehen schweigend um die lange Tischreihe und schreiben erfundene Klatschgeschichten unter die Namen.
Nachdem so ein Inventar des Klatsches erstellt ist, folgt der nächste Schritt: die SuS werden aufgefordert, den Raum, der für die Kommentare gelassen wurde, mit höflich bestimmten Erwiderungen zu füllen, die dem Verbreiter des Klatsches widersprechen soll.
Als Gesprächsstrategien sollten die SuS ggf. auf Möglichkeiten wie Widerspruch, Necken, Hinweis, warum etwas nicht stimmen kann, oder Änderung des Themas hingewiesen werden.
Als Musterbeispiel könnte Miss Maudies neckende Erwiderung an S. Crawford vorgelesen werden:
"Stephanie Crawford even told me once she woke up in the middle of the night and found him looking in the window at her. I said what did you do, Stephanie, move over in the bed and make room for him? That shut her up a while."
Miss Stephanie Crawford darf darauf selbstverständlich einen weiteren Versuch machen, ihre Klatschge-

schichten an den Mann oder die Frau zu bringen. Und das wird wiederum kommentiert.

Diese Form des Dialogs ist recht vergnüglich. Alle SuS sind aktiv beteiligt und üben sich in Englisch geführten Dialogen. SuS analysieren damit die Nachbarschaftssituation und stellen sie aus einer neuen Perspektive dar. Sie üben darüber hinaus eine angelsächsische Form der *polite reply* ein, die als kulturelle Bereicherung ins eigene verbale Handlungsrepertoire übernommen werden kann.

Die Bögen mit den „Klatschgeschichten" werden am Ende der Doppelstunde an den Wänden als Wandzeitung aufgehängt.

Fragestellungen

What might Miss Stephanie have gossipped about these people?

Supposing you came across this kind of gossip. What could you say to Miss Stephanie to stop her talking like this?

> **Ergebnis**
> Do you really think so?
> Ah, I don't know.
> How very interesting.
> I see.
> I have never heard about that.
> Oh, really?
> What you don't say.

Modul 5 Equal rights (1) – All men are created equal – except for those with a dark skin (3–4 Stunden)

Methode

„Typisch schwarz?" In dieser Unterrichtsphase beleuchten die SuS einige hervorstechende Merkmale schwarzer Lebensgeschichte in den USA. Denn so gleich, wie die Verfassung es vorgibt, sind Schwarz und Weiß nicht. Obwohl sich seit Ende des Bürgerkriegs viel verbessert hat, ist das Thema noch immer aktuell. Nachdem die SuS im 4. Modul Scouts Perspektive der Welt erarbeitet haben, vertiefen sie sich also jetzt in das zweite große Thema des Romans, die Rassentrennung. In der – fakultativen – ersten Stunde vergleichen SuS Geschichten mit „typisch schwarzen" Merkmalen: Mythen, Aberglauben, Hexengeschichten und moderne Großstadtmythen, und klären die Frage: Gibt es typisch schwarze Eigenschaften? – In der nächsten Doppelstunde berichten die SuS einander anhand historischer (oral history) und literarischer Dokumente, wie Sklaverei im Alltag aussah. Dabei benutzen sie WPA *(Work Progress Administration)*- Dokumente aus der Kongressbibliothek in Washington, die in den 30er Jahren erstellt wurden. – In der letzten Stunde recherchieren die SuS die Phasen der amerikanischen Bürgerrechtsbewegung und machen eine Expertenrunde: was auf dem Papier garantiert war, musste im politischen Kampf erst mühsam erobert werden. *To Kill a Mockingbird* ist eine Sprosse auf der Stufenleiter dieses Kampfes.

Fakultatives Unterthema: Myth-and-Witchcraft stories (1-2 Stunden)

Lernziele

Anhand von Aberglaube, Mystizismus und Geisterbeschwörung ein Verständnis der Kultur der Schwarzen in den 30er Jahren gewinnen.

Erkennen, dass einige Elemente dieses Glaubens nicht auf Schwarze und das letzte Jahrhundert beschränkt, sondern immer noch gültig sind.

Methode

Dies ist eine Zusatzstunde, in der Erzählfähigkeit und –freude ihren Platz haben. Zum Süden gehören Geschichten, und das Geschichtenerzählen selbst gehört auch dazu. Eine der berühmtesten Geschichten aus dem Süden ist die von Huckleberry Finn – übrigens eine sehr präzise linguistische und soziologische Momentaufnahme aus den 1880er Jahren: ein *white trash–kid* und ein entlaufener Negersklave (so Mark Twain selbst) machen sich auf, den American Dream des genussvollen in-den-Tag-Hineinlebens zu verwirklichen. Hexerei und Übersinnliches gehörte zur Welt der

Schwarzen 1933 genauso wie 1884. Unverstandene und unheimliche Wirklichkeitserfahrung wird darin zu Gruselgeschichten mit einem Schuss Aberglaubenweisheit verarbeitet, was ihren besonderen Reiz ausmacht. Aber sind wir heute so viel aufgeklärter?

In dieser Stunde erzählen die SuS einander Mythen aus drei Quellen. Sie stammen 1. aus Huckleberry Finn (die Szene, in der Tom, Huck und der Schwarze Jim sich gemeinsam über einen „Neger" lustigmachen, der, wie er meint, immer von Hexen geplagt wird), 2. aus To Kill a Mockingbird und 3. aus jüngster Zeit.

Wenn nur 45 Minuten zur Verfügung stehen, sollten die drei Arbeitsbögen zuvor als Hausaufgabe bearbeitet werden. Die Stunde hat ein doppeltes Ziel: 1. erzählen die SuS so viel wie möglich Geschichten mit einem unwahrscheinlichen Kern. Geschichten aus dem Süden. Geschichten aus dem heutigen Alltag. Sie lachen und lauschen und erfahren sinnlich das Vergnügen, unerhörte Geschichten zu hören und zu erzählen. Sie dürfen sich ungestört warmreden, wozu ja häufig die Zeit im Unterricht fehlt.

Dazu bereiten die SuS in drei Expertengruppen mit Untergruppen A, B, C etc. entsprechend der Klassenstärke ihre Geschichten vor:

1	Huck	A	B	C	D	E
2	Mockingbird	A	B	C	D	E
3	Modern Myths	A	B	C	D	E

Im Gruppenpuzzle tauschen die Experten dann untereinander ihre Geschichten aus.

2. Ziel der Stunde ist die kritische Reflexion über die Frage, ob das Vergnügen an *Myths and Witchcraft Stories* tatsächlich eine typisch schwarze Eigenschaft ist. Dies wird im UG zum Abschluss diskutiert. Dabei wird klar, dass die scheinbar typisch „schwarze" Eigenschaft, für Aberglaube, Mystizismus und Geisterbeschwörung anfällig zu sein, auf alle Menschen zutrifft.

Fragestellung

Are there any differences between white and black cultures? If yes – what are they?

Ergebnis
- white and black music
- rap
- jazz
- blues
- superstition, voodoo, witchcraft, myths

Methode

Anschließend lernen die SuS verschiedene Geschichten mit Elementen von Aberglauben und Legenden kennen. Die SuS lesen dazu zunächst die ihnen zugeteilten Texte (**KV 14** Adventures of Huckleberry Finn, myths and witchcraft – for very advanced students; **KV 15** Myths, find examples in Mockingbird; **KV 16** Modern Myths) zu Hause – oder im Unterricht in Gruppen –, und klären dann innerhalb der Expertengruppen die Verständnisfragen und bearbeiten die Aufgaben. Später beim Gruppenpuzzle sollen sie so viele verschiedene Geschichten wie möglich hören und (weiter-)erzählen. Dabei erfahren sie das Vergnügen an schrägen Geschichten am eigenen Leibe (= eigene Anfälligkeit für Mythen).

Fragestellung

Which elements make myths and witchcraft stories believable or effective?

Ergebnis
- Tom, Huck, and *nigger* Jim make the *nigger* believe he is followed by witches: black myth, but one black man is fooling another → self-doubt and fear
- Boo eats squirrels → frightening story
- Boo eats cats → frightening story
- Boo drives scissors into his Dad's thigh → frightening story
- vanished hitchhiker → inexplicable, strange, frightening
- white alligators in NY sewer system → strange, frightening
- dead Turklebaum → seemingly possible
- the stolen kidney → seemingly possible

Fragestellung

What kind of conclusions can you draw from your experience of telling those stories?

Ergebnis
- telling a story where somebody else is the naive fool, makes you feel superior
- whites like to ascribe superstition to blacks
- myths and witchcraft stories are not a typical black trait but universal

Modul 5

Unterthema: Rassismus in den USA – Der Sklavenstaat und sein Vermächtnis (2 Stunden)

Lernziel

Persönliche Einzelansichten aus dem Alltag von Sklaverei und Rassendiskriminierung (1852-1939) erzählen, hören, verstehen und historisch-politisch einordnen.

Methode

In dieser Doppelstunde vermitteln die SuS einander ein plastisches, visuelles Bild vom Alltag des Sklavenstaats und der Rassentrennung. Sie benutzen dazu historische und literarische Quellen. Die so gewonnenen Eindrücke setzen sie zur Welt der Schwarzen in *To Kill a Mockingbird* in Beziehung.

Um die Frage „Was macht das Leben zu Bedingungen der Rassendiskriminierung im Alltag aus?" beantworten zu können, referieren sie mit Hilfe von authentischem Photomaterial und einem Basisvortrag.

Die Doppelstunde funktioniert am besten, wenn die SuS die von ihnen gewählten Texte zu Hause erarbeiten und dann in einem *Kugellager* einander berichten. Insgesamt enthalten die beiden Kopiervorlagen Material für vier unterschiedliche Gruppengespräche und zwei Kurzreferate. Eine Binnendifferenzierung ist hier gut möglich. Die leistungsstärksten SuS arbeiten mit **KV 18.1 und 18.2** *Uncle Tom's Cabin, Ch XII*. Dieser Textauszug schildert drastisch eine Versteigerungsszene auf dem Sklavenmarkt, bei dem eine schwarze Mutter von ihrem Sohn getrennt wird. Da sehr viel Dialekt vorkommt, ist der Text nicht auf Anhieb und einfach zu lesen, dürfte aber für sehr gute SuS kein Problem darstellen.

Drei weitere Texte auf **KV 17.1** bis **17.3** *Racial segregation* sind einfacher zu verstehen. Sie entstammen der von Roosevelt initiierten WPA (Work Progress Administration)-Dokumentation des Nationalen Erbes. Damals, in den frühen 30er Jahren, lebten noch viele Schwarze, die als Kinder Sklaven gewesen waren. Die Interviews mit ihnen, ebenfalls linguistisch getreu transkribiert, haben eine hohe Authentizität. Sie sind heute in der Kongressbibliothek archiviert und online zugänglich. Man sieht die Menschen mit ihrem leidgeprüften Lebensschicksal beinahe vor sich, so ergreifend sind ihre Lebensberichte.

Die erste der sechs Gruppen hält eine Bildpräsentation (PowerPoint oder OHP – einige Schilder und Bilder sind kontrastreich genug um auch auf Folien ohne Graustufen zu wirken) mit Photos von Schildern aus den 30er Jahren, die den Schwarzen jeweils gesonderte Eingänge oder Plätze zuweisen (Photoabteilung der Library of Congress). Die Bilder werden erläutert und kommentiert (siehe **KV 17.1**).

Die 2. Gruppe hält einen kurzen Vortrag zum Thema „Rassentrennung" nach dem englischen Wikipedia-Eintrag (**KV 17.1**).

Anschließend an die beiden Einführungsvorträge klären SuS gemeinsam die Frage, wie ein Leben im Sklavenstaat, dessen Vermächtnis die Rassentrennung gewesen ist, aussah. Das wird am deutlichsten am Beispiel selbsterzählter oder selbsterlebter Episoden, die für ein ganzes Leben prägend wirkten. Dazu stehen nach der häuslichen Vorbereitung vier Lebensberichte zur Verfügung, die sich SuS nun gegenseitig erzählen. Sie bilden dazu ein *Kugellager*, doch sprechen sie nicht nur mit dem Gegenüber, sondern bilden Vierergruppen.

Die Gruppen 3 bis 5 haben die drei Texte von **KV 17** vorbereitet.

Gruppe 3 berichtet über einen oder mehrere ehemaligen Sklaven, die 1936-1938 als hochbetagte Menschen (bis zu 112 Jahre alt) interviewt wurden und bewegend aus ihrem Leben erzählen.

Gruppe 4 berichtet von einem 14jährigen schwarzen Pferdejungen, der um Haaresbreite einem Lynchmord entging.

Gruppe 5 berichtet von einem weiteren solchen Lebensschicksal: einer Schwarzen, deren Großvater in Afrika als Junge gestohlen und versklavt wurde.

Gruppe 6 hat **KV 18** *Uncle Tom's Cabin, Ch XII*. vorbereitet und berichtet von einer Versteigerungsszene auf dem Sklavenmarkt. Drastisch wird klar, was es hieß, wenn Familienmitglieder auf dem Sklavenmarkt voneinander getrennt wurden.

Vermittels Empathie erlangen SuS ein eindringliches Verständnis für das Leben der Schwarzen während Sklaverei und Rassentrennung.

Fragestellung

How did life of black Americans differ between times of slavery and the 1930's?

Ergebnis

Slavery

- import of black people from Africa – like chattel
- people sold, let and hired like things
- families separated
- work all day during daylight
- house and field negroes
- constitutional promises not fulfilled

Segregation

- special quarters in town for blacks
- black schools
- no interracial marriages
- special entrances in shops, bars, restaurants
- black churches
- black galleries in courts, cinemas, theatres
- black drinking fountains
- black park benches
- black areas in buses
- no admission to universities
- no right to vote

Modul 5

Methode

In Abschlussgespräch erörtern die SuS die Wirkung derartiger Alltagszustände auf spätere Generationen.

Fragestellung

What do you think were the effects of slavery and segregation on the attitudes of black and white Americans in the 1930s?

Ergebnis
- two class-society
- contempt for the blacks
- hatred against whites
- feelings of revenge on both sides
- fear of being killed
- grudge against judical system
- racial uproar
- *Mockingbird*-times nearer to slavery
- wound in society still not healed

Unterthema: Die Bürgerrechtsbewegung (1 Stunde)

Lernziel

Stufen des Kampfes um Gleichberechtigung erkennen, benennen und in ihrer Relevanz einordnen.

Methode

SuS haben gruppenweise zu Hause Kurzpräsentationen nach **KV 19** *Steps in the Civil Rights Movement* erarbeitet.
Vom Negersklavenstaat bis zum ersten schwarzen Präsidenten der Vereinigten Staaten haben viele Stufen geführt. Die verfassungsmäßig zugestandenen Rechte mussten sich die Schwarzen hart erkämpfen. Die in *To Kill a Mockingbird* beschriebene Zweiklassenjustiz am Beispiel des Tom-Robinson-Prozesses ist auch eine Station des Bürgerrechtskampfes.
Vor der Präsentation der Gruppenreferate sollten die Schüler ihr Wissen über wichtige Ereignisse in der Geschichte der Schwarzen in den USA und der Bürgerrechtsbewegung aktivieren.
Anschließend schildern die SuS in den vorbereiteten Referaten einige Ereignisse, die als Meilensteine in die Geschichte der Bürgerrechtsbewegung eingegangen sind.
Zu jedem Referat könnte auch ein kurzes Video gezeigt werden – die Ereignisse sind auf YouTube hervorragend dokumentiert; die Videos lassen sich leicht in eine PowerPoint-Präsentation einbauen.

Fragestellung

Which important stages of black American history and the civil rights movement do you know?

Ergebnis
- 1619 First Africans brought to Virginia
- 1861 Confederate States separate from Union and found the Confederacy. Beginning of Civil War. Main Issue: Slavery
- 1862 President Abraham Lincoln declares all slaves in the States of Confederacy to be free as of 1863
- 1868-1870 14th and 15th Amendmends to the constitution guarantee civil rights to all Afro-Americans
- 1939 Billie Holiday sings *Strange Fruit*
- 1954 Supreme Court declares racial segregation at schools against constitution
- 1955 Arrest of Rosa Parks; Montgomery Bus Boycott until 1956
- 1963 Martin Luther King's speech *I have a Dream* with its vision of equal rights
- 1964 Civil Rights Act signed by President Lyndon B. Johnson
- 1965 Bridge in Selma
- 1965 Assassination of Malcolm X; Voting Rights Act
- 1967 Thurgood Marshal becomes first black Judge at the Supreme Court
- 1968 Assassination of Martin Luther King
- 2005 Condoleezza Rice is first black *and* female Secretary of State
- 2009 Barack Obama first black American President

Methode

In einem weiteren Schritt sollen die SuS versuchen, die aufgeführten Ereignissse zu bewerten, indem sie sie nach Wichtigkeit in eine Reihenfolge bringen und dies begründen und diskutieren.
(Nach diesem Modul sollten die SuS die Voraussetzungen zum Schreiben von **Klausur A** haben, der Interpretation eines authentischen Ex-Sklavinnenberichts.)

Fragestellung

Which, do you think were the most important milestones in black/African American history and the civil rights movement?

Modul 6 Atticus' Plädoyer als politische Rede (3–6 Stunden)

Lernziel
Atticus' Plädoyer im Kontext historischer amerikanischer Reden verstehen.

Methode
In diesem Modul steht der Umgang mit einer Rede in der Tradition des demokratischen Liberalismus im Mittelpunkt. Von der klassischen zweiminütigen *Gettysburg Address* zieht sich der historische Faden über Martin Luther King's *I had a dream*-Rede über Atticus' Plädoyer bis hin zu Barack Obamas Siegesrede am 4. November 2008. Dieselben Themen werden in stets aktualisierter Form eindringlich ausgedrückt: die Idee, dass das Volk nach den Grundprinzipien des Liberalismus seinen eigenen idealen Staat errichtet hat und gegen Gefährdungen von außen verteidigt. Die Wirklichkeit der jeweiligen politischen Realität kontrastiert mit diesem Idealbild in oft drastischer Form.
(Im Anschluss an dieses Modul sind die SuS befähigt, die 2. Klausur zu schreiben, in der sie Obamas Siegesrede analysieren können.)

Unterthema: Gettysburg Address (Lincoln 19.11.1863) (2 Stunden)

Lernziel
Wichtige rhetorische Elemente zeigen und das Thema erkennen.

Methode
Die Analyse einer Rede setzt voraus, dass die SuS die formalen Merkmale einer Rede identifizieren und wirkungsästhetisch einordnen können. Diesem Aspekt sind die ersten 30 Minuten der Stunde gewidmet. Zunächst wird das Wissen der SuS über Kriterien, nach denen die Wirksamkeit einer Rede beurteilt werden kann, aktiviert. Danach finden die SuS mit Hilfe der **KV 20** in Gruppen selbst Beispiele für rhetorische Elemente.

Fragestellungen
What makes a speech a good one?
How can a speaker increase the effect of a speech?

Ergebnis
- catches one's interest
- sounds improvised, personal
- speaker talks to listeners' hearts
- easy, relaxed tone
- message
- sets free one's own energy
- → language as the medium of the message uses rhetorical devices

Methode
Danach gibt der L die Einführung zu den historischen Umständen der Gettysburg Address, wie oben auf **KV 21** *The Gettysburg Address* ausgeführt. L liest die Rede selbst oder lässt sie von sehr gutem SoS vortragen.
Die SuS analysieren die *Gettysburg Address* in EA selbständig. Dabei verwenden sie auch den 2. Teil der **KV 20** und versuchen neben den rhetorischen Mitteln die Struktur der Rede zu beschreiben (Markierungsstifte verwenden; rhetorische Elemente an den Rand schreiben; Zeit ca. 35 min).
Statt einer ausschließlich zentralen Auswertung im UG schlage ich zunächst eine Auswertung im Kugellager vor. Sie gibt jedem SoS die Gelegenheit sich zu artikulieren; zusätzliche Ideen der Gesprächspartner können ohne Gesichtsverlust mit aufgenommen werden.

Fragestellung
Which of the rhetorical means we know does Lincoln use and which does he not employ?

Ergebnis
Structure
- **Introduction** (1st para): Lincoln wins his listeners
  - all present have same fathers
  - commitment to great ideas dates back to those fathers
  - their great idea: equality
- **Present situation** (2nd para):
  - civil war
  - Has this nation a lasting chance in history?
  - Why are we all here? → consecrate a cemetery
- **Reasoning** (3rd para)
  - soldiers have consecrated cemetery in battle
  - soldiers' sacrifice will not be forgotten
  - their aims: survival of the nation; government = people
- **Peroration/Call for action** (3rd para)
  - we must carry on their unfinished work
  - keep nation alive
- → Lincoln combines reasoning and call for action.

Rhetorical devices

- *bring forth a nation:* metaphor
- *nation might live:* metaphor/personification
- *gave their lives ... nation might live:* antithesis
- *fitting and proper:* tautology
- *It is for us ... It is rather for us ...that from these ... that we here ... that these ... that this ...and that this:* anaphora
- *We are met ... We have come:* parallel structure
- *dedicate ... consecrate ... hallow ... of the people ... by the people ... for the people:* climax in 3 steps
- *little note, nor long remember:* alliteration
- *shall not perish:* litotes
- → Apart from using the metaphor of the nation as a living organism, Lincoln uses rhetorical means that repeat words and sounds to intensify his message.
- → L. doesn't use devices such as euphemism, exclamations, irony, onomatopoeia, because they would have been less appropriate.
- → Instead he uses highly emotional words (fathers, war, gave their lives, dedicate, consecrate, hallow, struggle, nobly, honored dead, freedom, died, earth) that contribute to the intensity of the message.

Aufgabe

Write a comprehensive interpretation of the Gettysburg Address including all the arguments you have found and heard from the others.

Fakultatives Unterthema   Martin Luther King's Speech *I have a dream* (2 Stunden)

Lernziel

Funktion der Redemittel darstellen und den Bezug auf große amerikanische Themen erkennen.

Methode

Die SuS können in der berühmten *I have a dream*-Rede von Martin Luther King (MLK) noch einmal die Elemente entdecken, die sie in Lincolns Rede herausgefunden haben. Die Rede steht in viererlei Aspekten in direkter Tradition Lincolns: sie wurde 100 Jahre nach Lincoln gehalten; sie wurde vor dem Lincoln Monument in Washington gehalten, und der in Stein gemeißelte Lincoln konnte MLK und die Demonstranten sehen; sie wurde ebenfalls vor einer Rekordmenge von Zuschauern gehalten – 250.000 –; sie führt inhaltlich den Gedanken des demokratischen Liberalismus fort und treibt ihn rhetorisch auf die Spitze.

MLK artikuliert sich nicht in staatsmännischer Kürze wie Lincoln. Dennoch ist es eine der berühmtesten amerikanischen Reden.
Die SuS sollten den Text **KV 22** vorbereitend lesen und im Unterricht die Leitfrage unter Verwendung ihres Wissens über Redeaufbau und Redemittel in Gruppen erarbeiten. Die Gruppen sollten dann die Schwerpunkte ihrer Ergebnisse berichten, wobei die später berichtenden Gruppen aufgefordert sind, nur noch neue Aspekte einzubringen.

Fragestellung

What makes Martin Luther King's speech "one of the great American speeches"?

Ergebnis

Structure

- **Introduction** (1st para) stressing the uniqueness of the occasion
- **Present situation** (paragraphs 3-5) MLK compares the present political situation of black Americans with the constitutionally guaranteed rights of equality and freedom. He urges black community to "cash" their "cheque" → their constitutional rights
- **Reasoning** (paragraphs 6-12)
- – No rest without full citizenship rights for blacks.
- – Appeal for peaceful struggle.
- – Appeal to continue until blacks are given full justice.
- **Peroration** (paragraphs 23, 24)
- – *let freedom ring*
- – *we are free at last*

Rhetorical devices

- anaphora and repetition: *One hundred years later ...; we refuse to believe...; Now is the time ...;We can never be satisfied ...; go back to ...;I have a dream ...; With this faith ...; Let freedom ring ...; when ... when ... when; every village, every hamlet, every state, every city; Free at last ...*
- parallel structure: *to work together, to pray together, to struggle together, to go to jail together, to stand up for freedom together...*
- metaphors
- – of light and dark: *e. g. beacon light of hope; flames of injustice; night of captivity; dark and desolate*
- – of sea and land: *e. g. lonely island of poverty; vast ocean of material prosperity; quicksands of racial injustice; rock of brotherhood; stone of hope*
- – of world of finance: *e. g. cash a check; bank of injustice; insufficient funds; great vaults of opportunity; richtes of freedom; poverty – prosperity*

- of nature: *whirlwinds of revolt; bright day of justice; heat of injustice; heat of oppression; oasis of freedom and justice; thirst for freedom*
- musical: *symphony of brotherhood; let freedom ring*
- of architecture: *architects of our republic; palace of justice; foundations of our nation*
- biblical: *God's children; day of justice*
- antithesis: *dark and desolate valley of segregation – sunlit path of racial injustice; daybreak – night; Negro community – white brothers; their destiny – our destiny; their freedom – our freedom; rightful place – wrongful deeds; sons of former slaves – sons of former slave owners; black boys – black girls; white boys – white girls; sisters and brothers; black and white; Jews and Gentiles; Protestants and Catholics*
- climax: *Negro is not free …, is sadly crippled …, is still languishing; life, liberty, and the pursuit of happiness; walk – march ahead – cannot turn back; every village – every hamlet – every state; free – free – free at last!*
- simile: *justice rolls down like waters; rightousness like a mighty stream*
- litotes: *I am not unmindful of …*
- chiasm: *Let freedom ring from every hill and molehill of Mississippi. From every mountainside, let freedom ring.*
- exclamation: *Free at last!*

→ The strongest rhetorical features are the **imagery** and **repetitions/rhythm** that carry the message and reinforce it.

Message
A political vision of racial equality based on the constitution and the American Dream → like a religious epiphany.
→ One of the great American speeches, because it combines great rhetorical skills, with classical American themes and a message of brotherhood and equality.

Lernziel
Erkennen, dass die Vortragsweise bei einer Rede eine weitere Dimension ist, die ihre letztendliche Wirkung ausmacht.

Methode
Die Rede sollte, wenn dazu irgendwie die Möglichkeit besteht, unbedingt im Anschluss an die Analyse gemeinsam angeschaut oder angehört werden. Auf diese Weise erleben die SuS am unmittelbarsten, dass eine (rein rationale) Analyse des gedruckten Wortes nicht alle Wirkungselemente einer Rede erfassen kann. Artikulation, Intonation und Emotionalität des Sprechenden im Zusammenwirken mit dem Gruppenerlebnis (auch im Klassenraum!) können bei Reden extrem verstärkend wirkend.

Fragestellung
What are the differences between the written and the spoken word?

Ergebnis
- African American gospel songstress
- effect of timing and pauses
- communication between audience and speaker
- influence of situation and location

Aufgabe
Write a detailed interpretation of MLK's speech. Analyse the speech and its effect and contrast it with Lincoln's speech.

Unterthema: Atticus' Plädoyer (1 Stunde)

Lernziel
In den rhetorischen Mitteln seines Plädoyers die Verwandtschaft zu politischen Reden erkennen.

Methode
In Atticus' Schlussplädoyer ist der Bezug auf Lincolns *Gettysburg Address* unübersehbar: er ruft Freiheit, Gleichheit und Gerechtigkeit im Namen der amerikanischen Verfassung an. Auch die geistige Nähe zu MLK wird deutlich – dessen Rede sollte nur 3 Jahre nach der Veröffentlichung des Romans gehalten werden. Atticus trifft also den Geist einer Zeit, die reif war, ihre Rassentrennung aufzugeben, die auf dem Papier ohnehin nicht mehr bestand. Er spannt den Bogen von den Menschenrechten und Bürgerrechten zur praktizierten Ungerechtigkeit in meisterhafter Kürze und Eleganz.
Er weiß, seit ihn der Richter mit der Übernahme des Falls betraut hat, dass er juristisch auf verlorenem Posten steht. Ihm geht es um die Menschenrechte überhaupt. Er statuiert ein Exempel am Beispiel des Robinson-Prozesses.
Ohne Umschweife häuft Atticus Argument auf Argument und legt damit die Verantwortung für die Amerikanische Verfassung auf die Schultern der Jury. Sein Stil ist äußerst ökonomisch und elegant. Nie denkt man darüber nach, dass er überhaupt irgendwelche Stilmittel verwendet, so stark zieht er seine Zuhörer in seinen Bann. Die Ökonomie seiner Wortwahl erzielt die Wirkung.

Modul 6

Inhaltlich widmet sich nur das halbe Plädoyer dem eigentlichen Gerichtsfall. Die zweite Hälfte hat den Charakter einer politischen Rede und ist ihr deshalb auch in den rhetorischen Mitteln besonders ähnlich.
Die SuS können den Aufbau der Rede und die wichtigsten Stilmittel nun zügig identifizieren. Sie isolieren sie in EA und vergleichen die Ergebnisse in den letzten 10 Minuten in einem Kugellager (zur Durchführung vgl. Modul 4).
Erweiternd könnte der L die SuS noch dazu befragen, wie das Plädoyer auf sie gewirkt hat, wie sie vermuten, dass es auf die Geschworenen gewirkt haben mag und mit welchen Argumenten sie diskutiert haben mögen. Nach diesem Modul sind die SuS hinreichend vorbereitet, die *Victory Speech* von Barack Obama (4. November 2008) als weiteres Glied in der Kette dieser drei Reden zu interpretieren. Sie ist Gegenstand der Klausur B. (siehe Anhang)

Fragestellung
How does Atticus try to convince the jury?

Ergebnis
Structure

- **Introduction (224 1-4)** addresses the jury politely and like a member of the family: eye level. No attitude of superiority.
- **Present situation (224 5-18)**
  - the case is clear
  - no evidence of a crime
  - defendant not guilty
- **Reasoning**
  The case:
  - psychological explanation of Mayella's behaviour: she kissed a negro and wanted to destroy the evidence (**224** 23-**225** 11)
  - explanation of Bob Ewell's behaviour and possible guilt (**225** 12-22)
  - the witnesses rely on the assumption that the jury will believe them more than a black man (**225** 23-36)
  Atticus moral and political convictions:
  - negative attitudes are common in the human race, not just in blacks (**226** 1-8)
  - praise of the Constitution: all men are created equal (**226** 15)
  - not equal in talents, funds, abilities, intelligence – but in court, which represents the constitution, they are equal (**226** 20-**227** 3)
- **Peroration** Invocation of the jury to do their duty
  - to realize the content of the Constitution in court (**227** 6-13)

Rhetorical means
- Anaphora: *... that all Negroes lie, that all Negroes are basically immoral beings, that all Negro men are not to be trusted around our women...; ... a lie as black as Tom Robinson's skin, a lie I do ...; ... some Negroes lie, some Negroes are immoral, some Negro men must not be trusted around women ...*
- Antitheses/Climax: *black and white; stupid and smart; idle and industrious; rich and poor; ignorant and intelligent* →: all-encompassing, giving a general meaning to his case.
- Chiasm: *You know the truth, and the truth is this. A court is only as sound as its jury, and a jury is only as sound as the men who make it up* → direct address of jury
- Simile: *a lie as black as Tom Robinson's skin*
- Final invocation: *In the name of God*
- Litotes: *I'm no idealist* → I know very well
- sparing use of metaphors: *the equal of a Rockefeller; the equal of an Einstein; the equal of any college president; courts are great levellers*

Message
- everything has been explained
- the case is clear
- the case is a test of the constitution
- → 1st part of Atticus' address to the jury gives psychological and logical evidence in the case. 2nd part presents moral and political convictions, uses more rhetorical devices and is more similar to a political speech.

Aufgabe
Compare Atticus's final speech to one of the other two speeches you have analysed (Lincoln or MLK).

Fakultative Zusatzstunde *Just a minute* (1 Stunde)

Lernziel
Spiel: Eine eigene Rede nach festgelegten Regeln und Themen halten.

Methode
Nach dem kognitiven Analysieren (Belastung der linken Hirnhälfte) halten die SuS nun selbst eine Rede (Belastung der rechten Hirnhälfte). Sie erhalten eine Stunde Rhetorikunterricht, verpackt in das Spiel *Just a minute*, das sich als Dauererfolgssendung auf BBC Radio Four seit über 40 Jahren großer Beliebtheit erfreut.
Hintergrund: 1967 Jahren fiel dem Londoner Ian Messiter im Obergeschoss eines Bus Nr. 13 ein, wie ihm

sein Lehrer die schreckliche Aufgabe gestellt hatte, eine einminütige Rede ohne Verzögerungen, Wiederholungen und Abschweifungen zu halten. Produzent David Hatch machte daraus eine Pilotsendung. Der BBC-Entwicklungsausschuss bezweifelte, dass die Serie mehr als sechs Sendungen überstehen würde.

Das Konzept der Sendung ist einfach. Vier prominente Kandidaten haben den Auftrag, eine Minute lang ohne Ähs und Emms, ohne verzögernde Pausen (*no hesitation*), Wortwiederholung (*no repetition*) oder Abschweifung (*no deviation*) eine Rede zu einem Begriff zu halten, der aber selbst nicht genannt werden darf. Die Einfachheit dieser Spielregeln hat dieser Sendung zum Dauererfolg verholfen. http://www.bbc.co.uk/radio4/comedy/justaminute.shtml

Das Sendeformat lässt sich leicht ins Klassenzimmer übertragen. Rhetorik ist curricular in keinem Unterrichtsfach vorgesehen, Überschneidungen sind also nicht zu erwarten. Es macht den SuS meist großen Spaß, in Form eines Klassenwettbewerbs eine Rede zu halten. Sie unterschätzen die Schwierigkeit der Aufgabe, gehen voller Selbstsicherheit heran und scheitern oft schon nach der ersten Sekunde an ihrem einleitenden „Äh". Das führt zu großer Abwechslung, einem hohen Lach- und Lerneffekt und staunender Einsicht über die eigene Redekultur. Da das Sprechen ja überwiegend unbewusst (rechte Hirnhälfte!) geschieht, also auf den Gegenstand selbst konzentriert ist, nicht aber auf die rhetorische Ausführung, muss auch seine Korrektur auf unbewusster Ebene stattfinden. Dafür ist das Spiel ***Just a minute*** optimal geeignet.

Der L teilt die Klasse nun nach dem Zufallsprinzip in Vierergruppen ein. Die ersten 4 SuS treten vor die Klasse. Ziel des Spiels ist, den besten Redner der vier zu ermitteln.

Der L stellt gut sichtbar eine Stoppuhr auf bzw. hält sie selbst in der Hand. Ein Teil des Witzes dieses Spiels kommt daher, dass die SuS das Thema erst recht kurz – je nach Leistungsstärke des Kurses – vor Beginn des Spiels erfahren.

Zur Erinnerung kann an die Tafel geschrieben werden: *no hesitation, no repetition, no deviation and don't mention the topic*

Weil der Sprecher sofort in einem Tonfall beginnt, als hätte er sich tagelang auf diese Rede vorbereitet, ist in der Regel schon der erste Satz sehr komisch.

Der Rest der Klasse achtet auf Regelverstöße. Sobald sie eintreten, ruft der erste, dem es auffällt: „*Hesitation!*", „*Repetition!*" oder „*Deviation!*" Dann drückt der L die Stoppuhr, analysiert kurz den Fehler und gibt dem Nächsten ein Zeichen. Dabei drückt er die Stopuhr auf „Weiter". Das erfordert ein wenig Übung. Eine Minute kann sich auf diese Weise sehr in die Länge ziehen. Der Redner, bei dem die Minute voll wird, gilt als Sieger. Alle rufen „*Hooray!*" Diese positive Bestätigung ist wichtig. Wenn alle SuS einmal an der Reihe waren, ist die Aufmerksamkeit für verzögerungsfreies Sprechen erfahrungsgemäß noch tagelang geschärft.

Themenideen für 1-Minuten-Reden:

The South	*Mixed marriages*
Father	*Dogs*
Daughter	*Guns*
The North Pole	*Mad dogs*
Mother	*My hobby*
Blacks	*Cats*
White people	*Whales*
Civil War	*Dolls*
Mockingbirds	*Donald Duck*
Penguins	*Smoking*
Swearing	*Cycling to school*
Typing blindly	*Reading*
Germany	*The American Constitution*
Orphans	*Mathematics*
The rose	*Computers*

Modul 7 Atticus the man – moralisches Vorbild und Ideal (3–4 Stunden)

Lernziel
Die Figur und Rolle des Atticus Finch erfassen und charakterisieren können.

Methode
Wie ist Atticus eigentlich? Ist er kalt und unnahbar? Oder ist er voll warmen Mitgefühls für die Unterprivilegierten? Versteht er etwas von Kindern oder überlässt er sie nur sich selbst? Hat er ein gesundes Gerechtigkeitsgefühl oder ist er ein Rechtsphantast wie Michael Kohlhaas? Wie sehen ihn die anderen Protagonisten? In einer Podiumsdiskussion loten die SuS seine Persönlichkeit aus.

In einer fakultativen Unterrichtseinheit machen sich die SuS Gedanken über wichtige Entscheidungssituationen, denen sich Atticus gegenübersieht und welche Handlungsspielräume er gehabt hätte.

Zur Abrundung halten die SuS in der dritten Stunde eine selbst entworfene kurze Tischrede auf Atticus.

Unterthema: Charakterisierung der Figur Atticus Finch (2 Stunden)

Lernziel
Die Person Atticus aus der Sicht der anderen Protagonisten ausleuchten.

Modul 7

Methode

Um nicht nur die Figur des Atticus Finch sondern auch seine Rolle (bzw. Funktion) im Roman zu verstehen, müssen die SuS betrachten, wie Atticus von den anderen Protagonisten wahrgenommen wird. Dazu bereiten sie mit Hilfe von **KV 23** *Atticus' personality traits* in sieben Gruppen Argumente vor, die unterschiedliche Aspekte seines Charakters betonen. Diese Liste kann bei Bedarf mit anderen Personen (z.B. Mrs Dubose, Sheriff Tate, Mrs Merriweather, Mrs Stephanie Crawford) und ihren Einschätzungen ergänzt oder geändert werden.

In der 2. Stunde bilden die SuS ein *Panel* mit je einem Mitglied aus jeder Gruppe. Der Diskussionsleiter eröffnet die Debatte mit der Frage *What do you think is the core of Atticus Finch's character?*

Die SuS arbeiten in ihren Beiträgen heraus, dass Atticus ein leuchtendes Beispiel ist für Bescheidenheit *(modesty)*, Gerechtigkeit *(sense of justice)*, Geradlinigkeit *(straightness)*, Gelassenheit *(calmness)*, Herzlichkeit *(warmth)*. Bei ihm gelten keine *double standards*.

Fragestellungen

How does the author manage to show Atticus from several perspectives?

What is the core of Atticus' character?

Ergebnis

1. Aunt Alexandra's view

Atticus
- has no idea how to bring up children
- lets the children run wild
- allows Scout to be a tomboy
- has no idea about how to raise a Finch daughter
- is a risk for the family honour
- allows children too much insight into his professional activity
- allows a black woman to be the sole educator of Scout

2. Jem's view

Atticus
- only sits and reads
- is reliable, but often remote
- is too old (nearly fifty) to play football or do interesting things that other fathers do
- is admirable for his modesty and sense of justice
- can put himself into other people's skins
- has courage and is self-controlled

3. Scout's view

Atticus
- is admirable
- can always be trusted
- gives physical and psychological warmth
- is the ultimate moral authority
- always gives good advice

4. Mr Underwood's view

Atticus
- is right in protecting Tom Robinson
- didn't stand a chance against the jury

5. Judge John Taylor's view

Atticus
- is the best lawyer to defend Tom Robinson
- is trustworthy
- will be able to bear the defeat
- is a patriot with a strong sense of justice

6. Mayella Ewell's view

Atticus
- feels superior and despises her
- scares her
- pretends to be polite
- is calculating and cold
- tries to expose her as a liar
- trusts a negro more than her

7. Mr Cunningham's view

Atticus
- is helpful and generous (not worried about receiving payment)
- is in the wrong defending and protecting a negro
- has the correct judgement of the court case
- is an authority

→ **The core of his character**
- modesty
- strong sense of justice
- straightness
- calmness
- warmth

Unterthema: Atticus' choices (1 Stunde)

Lernziel
Erkennen, dass Atticus in seiner Vorbildfunktion im Roman wenig Handlungsalternativen hat.

Methode
Die SuS erarbeiten im UG wichtige (und weniger wichtige) Entscheidungssituationen, denen Atticus ausgesetzt ist und formulieren Fragen nach alternativen Entscheidungsmöglichkeiten.
Anschließend werden jeweils ein bis zwei Fragen in kleineren Gruppen bearbeitet und diskutiert.

Fragestellung
Which important decisions does Atticus make in the novel and which alternative decisons could he have made?

Ergebnis

- Could Atticus have rejected the Robinson case?
- Could he have told Aunt Alexandra to stay in Finch's Landing?
- Could he have asked Aunt Alexandra not to intervene in Scout's upbringing?
- Should he have spared Jem the ordeal of reading to Mrs Dubose?
- Could he have asked Boo to see his children?
- Could he have come to an arrangement with Judge Taylor?
- Should he have been more worried about Bob Ewell's threats?
- Should he have insisted on a proper enquiry into the death of Bob Ewell?

→ Being the character that he is, he didn't have a lot of alternatives to what he decided to do.

Fakultatives Unterthema: Lobrede auf Atticus halten (1-2 Stunden)

Lernziel
Gemeinsames Erarbeiten und Vortragen einer Lobrede, wie sie in angelsächsischen Ländern gehalten wird.

Methode
Es ist nicht wahrscheinlich, dass die SuS jemals eine politische Rede oder einen Nachruf auf Englisch halten müssen. Eine launige Tischrede zu halten, mit Humor und einer Anekdote gewürzt, ist hingegen eine bei vielen Anlässen einsetzbare Fertigkeit. Gerade leichte, improvisiert klingende Reden kommen sehr gut an – und sind doch so viel schwerer zu halten als steife, langweilige Reden! Angelsachsen folgen in ihrer rhetorischen Konvention dabei gewissen unausgesprochenen Regeln, die wir im Folgenden darlegen. Die SuS sollen am Beispiel einer Tischrede zu Atticus' 60. Geburtstag diese Konventionen einmal exemplarisch anwenden.
Im UG entwickelt der L gemeinsam mit den SuS Kriterien für eine gute Tischrede. Die **KV 24** *Eulogy on Atticus* nimmt diese Elemente auf und strukturiert die Rede der SuS. Es empfiehlt sich, die Gruppengröße auf zwei bis drei SuS zu limitieren.
Zu der ausgewählten Eigenschaft erfinden die SuS einen Witz oder eine humoristische Begebenheit. Sie erzählen dies – schriftlich – so, dass der Witz zur Person von Atticus hinführt. Zeitvorgabe hierfür ca. 10 Minuten.
Vielleicht ist Scout gekommen? Vielleicht auch der Senator von Alabama? Wie heißt er/sie? Wie redet man ihn/sie an? („Dear Senator X"; oder „Dear Representative X") – zu weiteren Fragen des Protokolls siehe http://www.ushistory.org/Betsy/images/p600_60.pdf
Es sollte klar gemacht werden, dass kurze Tischreden möglichst frei zu halten sind und man das Ergebnis der Arbeitsgruppe deshalb einigermaßen auswendig lernen sollte. Natürlich sollten alle Reden vorgetragen werden. Die SuS können so auch die Reaktion auf den Inhalt und ihre Vortragsweise erfahren.
Sehr effektvoll ist es, wenn jeder ein Stielglas mitbringt, das, gefüllt mit Saft oder Wasser, zum Toast erhoben und geleert wird.

Fragestellung
What can be regarded as Atticus' typical qualities?

Ergebnis
- modesty
- strong sense of justice
- moral integrity
- calmness
- sense of humour
- good marksman
- deep understanding of his children

Modul 8 Equal rights (2) – Mann und Frau
(3 Stunden)

Lernziel

Die Rolle einer jungen Frau im amerikanischen Süden der 30er Jahre anhand des Frauenbilds im Roman verstehen.

Methode

Nicht nur Schwarze werden in den 30er Jahren als anders gehandelt, auch Frauen zählen zu den Wesen, die nicht gleich sind. Zwar dürfen sie wählen, aber der Verhaltenskodex schreibt für eine junge Dame des Südens ein bestimmtes Verhalten in einer von Männern getrennten Welt vor. Scout fühlt sich dadurch diskriminiert und eingeengt. In diesem Modul spüren die SuS diesen Veränderungen nach. Welche Regeln und Vorschriften sind das überhaupt, mit denen Scout da konfrontiert wird? (1. Stunde) Und wie – dies ist eine psychologische Fragestellung – entwickelt sich ihre Geschlechtsidentität als Frau (2. und 3. Stunde).

Unterthema: Frauenrollen im amerikanischen Süden – Identifikationsmodelle für Scout (1 Stunde)

Lernziel

Elemente und Aspekte der Mädchenerziehung in den Südstaaten der 1930er Jahre erkennen.

Methode

Wie fühlt sich die Ungleichbehandlung von Männern und Frauen aus der Sicht der heranwachsenden jungen Dame an? Scout muss auch in diese Haut schlüpfen, so wenig es ihr behagt. Die SuS erkunden das Rollenmodell der *Southern Belle* und das Frauenbild der 30er Jahre, das Scout erfüllen soll.
Als Ausgangspunkt für das Thema wird dabei der Begriff der *Southern Belle* durch Internetrecherche und/oder mit Hilfe der **KV 25** erarbeitet. Als zusätzliche Alternative böte sich an, dass einige SuS zuvor, eventuell gemeinsam, den 4 Stunden langen Film *Gone with the Wind* nach dem Roman von Margaret Mitchell ansehen. Er bietet zahlreiche Hinweise auf die Frauenrolle der *Southern Belle*. Besondere Aufmerksamkeit sollten die SuS Kostümierung, Aussehen, Kosmetik, Haarpflege, Verhalten und der geistigen Ausbildung schenken.
Im UG werden zunächst alle Aspekte zusammengetragen, die die *Southern Belle* ausmachen.
Dann erarbeiten die SuS im *place mat*-Verfahren, welche *Southern Belle*-Ideale noch in Aunt Alexandra's Erziehungsmaßstäben für Scout erkennbar sind.

Die Arbeit mit dem ‚Platzdeckchen' entstammt der Methodenkiste der sogenannten kooperativen Lernformen. Dabei arbeiten die SuS in Gruppen zu viert oder sechst an einem einzigen Thema. Die Aufgabe besteht darin, innerhalb einer gegebenen Zeitspanne gemeinsam eine Frage zu bearbeiten oder Lösungsvorschläge für ein Problem zu finden. Man nimmt dazu einen großen Bogen Packpapier oder unbedrucktes Zeitungspapier und teilt es so auf, dass jeder SoS ein kleines Areal für sich erhält. Es können also 6 SuS am Tisch sitzen und schreiben, ohne ihren Platz verlassen zu müssen.
Auf dem zugewiesenen Areal schreibt er/sie zunächst nieder, was ihm/ihr selbst zum Thema einfällt. Nach einer vorher vereinbarten Zeitspanne, z. B. 5 Minuten, werden die Einzelergebnisse vorgelesen, und die wichtigsten Ergebnisse noch einmal in der Mitte zusammengetragen.
Diese Präsentation eignet sich z. B. auch als Wandzeitung.

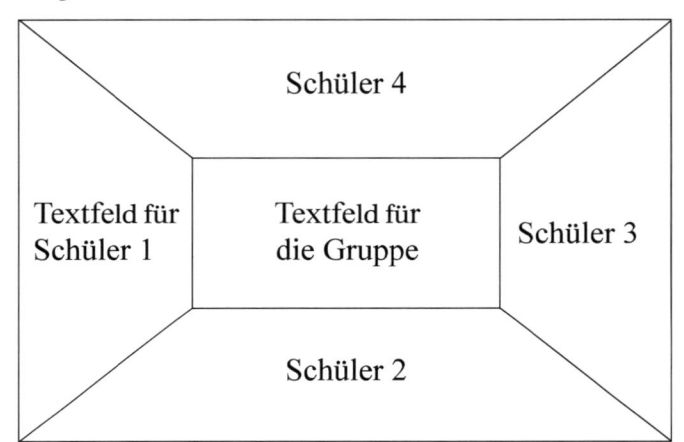

```
┌─────────────────────────────────┐
│          Schüler 4              │
│  ┌───────────────────────────┐  │
│Textfeld für│ Textfeld für │Schüler 3│
│Schüler 1   │ die Gruppe   │        │
│  └───────────────────────────┘  │
│          Schüler 2              │
└─────────────────────────────────┘
```

Place Mat für 4 SuS

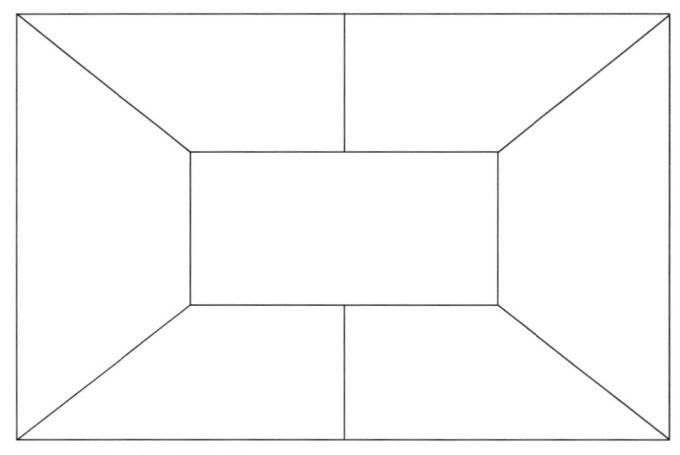

Place Mat für 6 SuS

Fragestellungen

What are the qualities of a 'Southern Belle'?

Which of these qualities are still reflected in Aunt Alexandra's way of bringing up Scout?

Ergebnis (Frage 2 in fett)

general situation
- **white**
- **no professional activity**
- **the husband earns the money**
- **stay mainly in the house**
- **have representative tasks**
- **organize ladies' activities**

behaviour
- **limited topics of conversation**
- **refined and sophisticated**
- riding in a ladies' saddle
- **be punctual and reliable**
- **use ladylike language**
- **class conceit**
- **be a model to one's daughters**

body posture
- **straight, upright (sitting, walking)**
- **wear delicate clothes**
- wear corsett (limited movements)
- **no trousers**

make-up and hairstyle
- **perfect at all times**

accepted activities
- **supervise household**
- **attend a missionary circle**

Unterthema: Das Frauenbild im Roman – Scouts sexuelle Identität (2 Stunden)

Lernziel
Die Stufen von Scouts sexueller Identität (=Frauwerdung) nachzeichnen.

Methode
In dieser Stunde werden die Ergebnisse der Vorstunde (Welche Rollenmodelle gab es für Scout?) in Bezug gesetzt zu Scouts tatsächlicher Entwicklung einer sexuellen Identität. Dies geschieht durch Erarbeitung einzelner Stadien in Gruppenarbeit und ein auswertendes abschließendes Unterrichtsgespräch. Tatsächlich vollzieht sich bei Scout eine Wandlung von einer anfänglichen männlichen Identität (*tomboy*) zu einer halbherzig akzeptierten Identität als künftige Dame am Ende des Romans.

Aufgrund der relativ komplexen Aufgabenstellung in der GA (**KV 26** *Stages of Scout's sexual identity*), kann auch in dieser Stunde noch einmal das *Place Mat*-Verfahren angewendet werden, wenn dies in der vorangegangenen Stunde erfolgreich verlaufen ist und das Verfahren gut dadurch eingeübt ist.

Fragestellungen

Is Scout still a tomboy at the end of the book?

In which stages does Scout's sexual identity develop?

Ergebnis

Group 1 – Summer 1933

- Relation to **Jem and Dill** → tomboy,
- – equal to Jem and Dill,
- – male identity.

- Relation to **Calpurnia** → constant quarrels,
- – does not accept Calpurnia as surrogate mother,
- – Cal expects a more feminine girl.

- Relation to **mother** → seems to have forgotten her,
- – does not bemoan her mother's death,
- – mother was gentle, feminine person,
- – does not identify with her.

Group 2 – Summer 1934

- Relation to **Jem and Dill** → boys separate,
- they regard her sexual identity as "different from ours",
- Scout does not feel different from them,
- still male identity,
- misunderstood by the boys,
- disappointed,
- feels the loss of the friendship,
- Dill's *engagement* does not really make up for the loss.
- Relation to **Miss Maudie** → disappointment, resignation, admiration,
- admiration of MM's male features,
- admiration of women's surplus work when doing household work,
- Scout can identify with this "male" kind of femininity.
- Difference **Miss Maudie Calpurnia**: Scout does not identify with Cal.

Group 3 – Summer 1935

- Scout suddenly realizes that Cal is a mother and Zeebo her son,
- she realizes that Cal has her own home,
- she wants to go and visit her home,
- she suddenly identifies with Calpurnia, a mother and housewife.
- Aunt Alex notices Scout's identification with Cal, too and tries to stop this,
- Calpurnia should not act as a role model for a young Southern Belle, Scout,
- Calpurnia can instil neither class consciousness nor racial pride in Scout,
- Aunt Alexandra thinks that only she herself can serve as a model for sexual identity.
- Aunt Alexandra's work: Scout's sexual identity,
- wear skirts all the time,
- be present at missionary's circle,
- learn the rituals of such ordeals: choice of guests, clothes, cakes, topics of conversation, opinions,
- Scout tries to meet her expectations,
- has some success.
- It is not a wholehearted identification; she thoroughly dislikes having to become a lady.

Group 4 – Summer 1935

- Father-daughter-relationship → Mayella is badly treated by her own father, Scout is loved like an adult person by her father; Scout's father takes care of her, Mayella's father uses her,
- father Atticus: loving, sexually distanced,
- father Bob: careless, drinks, neglectful yet usurpatory.
- Mother-daughter-relationship → both girls' mothers have died.
- Mayella has a strong feminine sexual identity; she desires Tom Robinson sexually.
- Scout is verbally engaged to Dill, but does not really understand what that means.
- she has no feminine sexual identity relating to men / boys,
- she has no inkling about the implications of sex,
- she cannot begin to understand the nature of Tom Robinson's alleged crime.
- Scout perceives Mayella Ewell as a witness in a trial, not as a woman,
- the offence of the trial is unfamiliar to her.

Group 5 – October 31, 1935

- Overalls → classic male garment, allows freedom of movement, carelessness, unisex.
- On the night after the crime Aunt Alex puts Scout's overalls on → she allows her a symbol of male sexual identity → gesture of reconciliation at the end of the book,
- after this, Scout can accept Aunt Alex as substitute mother.
- Boo und Scout together on the swing on the Finch porch: image of an old couple in their sunset years,
- both Boo and Scout have never developed a full sexual identity.
- Scout's sexual identity → final judgement:
- her maturity is that of a person who is no longer a child and can take on responsibility for others,
- Scout has not yet found her sexual identity at the end of the book,
- she has only found a negative identity → does not want to be like Aunt Alexandra, Miss Stephanie or the ladies of the missionary's circle.

Modul 9 Final discussion (4 Stunden)

Methode
Als Abschluss der gesamten Unterrichtsreihe bietet sich an, den Film anzusehen sowie in einer Podiumsdiskussion das Buch individuell zu evaluieren.

Unterthema: Der verfilmte Roman (4-5 Stunden)

Lernziel
Beurteilen und begründen können, ob die Filmversion dem Roman kongenial ist.

Methode
Die abschließende Bewertung des Romans soll Robert Mulligans Film von 1962 einleiten. Wegen der Überlänge des Films (129 Minuten) muss man Randstunden verwenden oder eine 3. Unterrichtsstunde hinzunehmen.
Es versteht sich von selbst, dass versucht werden sollte, den Film in möglichst großem Format zu sehen.
Als Einstellung empfiehlt sich die Kombination „englischer Ton" und „englische Untertitel", denn es braucht auch für geübte Zuschauer einige Zeit, bis man in den Alabama-Tonfall hineinfindet.
Vor dem Beginn des Films erhalten die SuS gruppenweise Aufträge aus dem *Viewing Log* (**KV 27**). Nach dem Betrachten sollten diese Arbeitsaufträge kurz schriftlich beantwortet werden, um sie in der anschließenden Stunde oder Doppelstunde im UG zu besprechen.

Ergebnis
- In particular, the events of part 1 of the book are condensed and limited to the central scenes. The trial in comparison is only slightly shortened.
- The cast helps to make the characters believable.
- The film conveys a similar balance of sentiment and intellect to the novel.
- The condensation of scenes and events in the film give it a different intensity to the novel. The loss of scenes and of the time span covered in the book lead to a loss of depth in the characters and detail in the children's environment.

Unterthema: Abschlussdiskussion (1 Stunde)

Lernziel
Themen des Romans bewerten und die Wirkung der Lektüre auf einen selbst und darlegen.

Methode
Das Projekt wird auf zweierlei Weise beendet:

- Die SuS schließen ihr Portfolio ab, das sämtliche schriftlichen Unterlagen einschließlich des Bildmaterials enthält.
- Mit einer Podiumsdiskussion.

Zum Abschluss des Projekts sollen die SuS eigene Eindrücke vortragen. Dazu erhalten sie die Themen von **KV 28** *Topics for a panel discussion* und suchen sich ein Thema aus, das ihnen und zwei oder drei Mitschülern/-innen gefällt. Nach individueller Vorbereitung der Argumente tragen die SuS ihre Meinung in Form einer Podiumsdiskussion vor. Die Moderation übernimmt ein jeweils vom L bestimmter weiterer Schüler. Bei schwächeren Gruppen kann der L auch selbst die Moderation übernehmen und das Gespräch steuern.

Die Themenangebote kreisen um die Bereiche

- growing up
- role of women
- injustice in court
- Atticus
- portrayal of good and evil in the novel
- scary subjects in modern media
- what I liked, what I didn't like in the novel
- the book's personal message for me

Die Themen sind so gewählt, dass die SuS eher zur Äußerung von Meinungen als zu sachlichen Stellungnahmen bewogen werden. Die Podiumsdiskussion läuft mit diversen Besetzungen ab. Die Teilnehmer diskutieren über ihre Rezeption des Romans und seiner Themen. Das Projekt ist damit beendet.

Zusatzmaterial (12 Stunden)

Lernziel
Wer den Unterricht mit der Betrachtung formaler Einzelaspekte vertiefen will, findet hier Zusatzmaterial für Einzelstunden, die sich problemlos jedem beliebigen Post-Reading-Modul zuordnen lassen: eine Doppelstunde, in der sich die SuS mit heftiger Kritik an *To Kill a Mockingbird* auseinandersetzen, eine Einzelstunde zur genaueren Betrachtung der Namensbedeutung im Roman; eine Einzelstunde zu Symbolen und Metaphern; eine Einzelstunde mit Anregungen für kreative Zusatzaufgaben sowie 3 Doppelstunden CLIL-Material, das sich in den Bereichen Biologie, Gemeinschaftskunde und Geschichte einsetzen läßt. Aber auch an den Bedarf der Profiloberstufe wurde dabei gedacht, wo themenübergreifendes Lernen Programm ist.

Zusatzthema: Rezeptionsgeschichte (2 Stunden)

Lernziel
Reaktionen auf *To Kill a Mockingbird* analysieren. Erarbeiten unterschiedlicher Positionen.

Methode
In den rund 50 Jahren seit seinem Erscheinen hat der Roman das ganze Spektrum der Kritik abbekommen. Vom höchsten Lob bis zu den Bedenken der politisch Korrekten, die sich an der Verwendung des Wortes *nigger* störten, von Rassenfanatikern auf der Linken, denen *Mockingbird* nicht liberal genug ist, bis zu Rassenfanatikern auf der Rechten, denen das gezeichnete Bild der US-Gesellschaft zu negativ ist, findet sich jede Meinung. Wir wollen den SuS einen aktuellen Zeitungsartikel und einen dazugehörigen Blog vorstellen und sie anregen, ein eigenes Urteil abzugeben.

Methode
Die SuS erhalten zunächst die **KV 29** *Harper Lee's novel is a racist morality tale – by Fred Leebron, Sep 14, 2007*. Der L erläutert im UG, dass es sich um einen relativ aktuellen Artikel handelt, der 2007 im *Seattle Post Intelligencer* erschien. Der *Seattle PI* war eine der beiden Tageszeitungen in Seattle, Washington und erschien seit 1863 täglich. Im März 2009 wurde nach 146 Jahren sein Erscheinen eingestellt. Die Zeitung ist nunmehr nur noch online zu erhalten. Sie gehört zur Hearst-Gruppe und gilt als liberal. – Fred Leebron ist ein (weißer) Hochschullehrer; er lehrt in Gettysburg. Die SuS sollen zunächst den Artikel einzeln in Stillarbeit lesen und die Positionen farblich markieren.

Fragestellung
What could people find to criticize about the novel these days?

> ### Ergebnis
> Fred Leebron's criticism:
>
> 1. Mockingbird → a morality tale which does not live up to its own standards → Hence it is bigotted.
> 2. Despite her alleged liberal opinion, the author portraits blacks as second-class citizens. Proof:
> - blacks are not even as articulate as 8-year-old Scout
> - blacks cannot think as clearly as 8-year-old Scout – blacks are portrayed as simpletons
> - Scout takes a superior position in her judgement about blacks → Tom's manners are described as good *in their own way*. → condescending; how would the child Scout know it all?
> 3. Secret message of the book → whites *are* superior. That's why it is so popular among whites.
> 4. White majority of the population is sinking drastically, yet Lee practices racism, even though she pretends to renounce it.

Methode
Danach schreiben die SuS zu jedem der Argumente ihre eigene Meinung auf und begründen diese.

Weitere Auswertung – Methode 1
Die SuS bestimmen den politischen Standort des Autors als *ultra conservative, conservative, liberal, extremely liberal* und begründen ihr Urteil im UG.

> ### Ergebnis
> - Fred Leebron gives an 'extremely liberal' opinion.
> - He condems a 50-year-old text for not conforming to a 20-year-old opinion.
> - Leebron's judgement is typical for 'politically correct people' who try and judge older works by applying modern standards.

Weitere Auswertung – Methode 2

Walk and Swap

Eine andere Form der Auswertung verwickelt die SuS stärker in Gespräche miteinander. Dazu kopiert der L die Vorlage **KV 30** *Walk and Swap – Leebron's Arguments* so häufig, dass jeder zweite SoS eine Karte erhält.
Auf diese Karte schreiben diese SuS <u>eines</u> der Leebron-Argumente. Auf die Rückseite schreiben sie ihre eigene Meinung dazu.
Nun gehen die SuS mit ihren Karten frei im Raum herum. Auf ein Signal des L („Stop!") wenden sie sich dem am nächsten Stehenden zu und zeigen zunächst das Leebron-Zitat. „What do you think?" Die andere SuS sagt ihre eigene Meinung, und nun tauschen die beiden ihre Meinungen aus.
Am Ende des Gesprächs wechselt die Karte ihren Besitzer. Nun geht der zweite SuS damit durch den Raum und sucht sich einen Partner, mit dem er/sie diskutieren kann. Jetzt wird das Gespräch schon länger:
"Leebron says …; A thinks …, I agree / disagree; what do you say?"
Am Ende der Diskussion wechseln die Karten abermals den Besitzer. So wandern die SuS durch den Klassenraum, bis sie alle Argumente einmal gehört und kommentiert haben.

Weitere Auswertung – Methode 3

Posting

Eine dritte Auswertung, die sich an die zweite anschließen kann, nimmt eine Form der Internetdebatte auf, die gemeinhin als *posting* bezeichnet wird. Darin wirft irgend jemand ein Argument in die Debatte und stellt es in einem Forum zur Diskussion. Zufällige Leser greifen das Argument auf und schreiben ihre Meinung dazu. Die Etikette besagt, dass man einander dabei nicht persönlich beleidigen darf.
Diese Form des Austauschs wird im Klassenraum imitiert. Auf anderen Tischen werden die Meinungskarten der Auswertung 2 auf ein DIN-A-3-Blatt geheftet und ausgelegt. Nun gehen die SuS von Tisch zu Tisch und fügen wie in einem Blog ihre eigene Meinung hinzu, bis ein regelrechtes Diskussionsforum entstanden ist.

Weitere Auswertung – Methode 4

Die SuS führen ein Rededuell, in dem sie ihre Meinung sowohl zu Leebron als auch ihre eigene Meinung zur *political correctness* des Buches diskutieren.

Aufgabe

Post your opinion on an article about *To Kill a Mockingbird* and print it out.

Zusatzthema: Die implizite Bedeutung von Namen (1 Stunde)

Lernziel

Namen als literarisches Ausdrucksmittel erkennen.

Methode

What's in a name? Mit diesem ‚verdeckten' Zitat aus *Romeo and Juliet* soll eine Diskussion über die verdeckte Bedeutung der im Roman verwendeten Namen angeregt werden. Die SuS erhalten das Arbeitsblatt **KV 31.1** *What's in a name?* mit den darin verzeichneten Arbeitsaufträgen, den phonetischen, onomatopoetischen, historischen und sonstigen Anspielungen assoziativ nachzugehen.
Die Stunde wird vermutlich am besten gelingen, wenn man sie im Computerraum durchführt und den SuS Gelegenheit gibt, die Fragen online zu bearbeiten.
Man kann sie aber auch als UG führen, nachdem die SuS zuvor Gelegenheit hatten, allein oder in Partnerarbeit ihre eigenen Gedanken zu den Namen zu erkunden.

> **Ergebnis**
>
> (siehe ausführliche Lösungsskizze **KV 31.2**)
>
> → The names are carefully chosen and create numerous allusions and associations.

Zusatzmaterial

Zusatzthema: Symbole und Metaphern (2 Stunden)

Lernziel

Die Wirkung von Symbolen und Metaphern erkennen.

Methode

Für diese Aufgabe kann man auch eine Einzelstunde verwenden; oder man spricht im Einzelfall immer wieder einmal einzelne Metaphern und Symbole an. Aufgrund der großen Anzahl an Symbolen und Metaphern im Roman ist es nicht sinnvoll, alle verwendeten Symbole und Metaphern aufzuführen. Die **KV 32.1** *Symbols and Metaphors* versucht, einige davon exemplarisch zu behandeln und die SuS auf deren verdeckte Bedeutungen zu bringen. Der Roman ist fast auf jeder Seite gespickt mit doppelten Bedeutungen. Man kann behaupten, dass nahezu jedes Objekt, jeder Name, jeder Ort, jeder Gegenstand eine versteckte doppelte Bedeutung besitzt. Die Rafinesse dieser literarischen Form liegt auf der Hand: wer die Zweitbedeutung *nicht* erkennt, fühlt sich dennoch gut unterhalten. Wer sie aber erkennt, freut sich über diesen Appell an den eigenen Bildungsgrad, über den Tiefsinn und die Bedeutungsfülle. Das ist auch einer der Gründe, warum man *To Kill a Mockingbird* mehrmals im Leben lesen kann und dabei jeweils neue Bedeutungsebenen entschlüsselt. Die Lektüre wird nie langweilig. Harper Lee ist auf eine intelligente Art unterhaltsam und auf eine unterhaltsame Weise intelligent, die ihresgleichen sucht.

Im UG wiederholen die SuS noch einmal, was sie über Symbole und Metaphern wissen (vgl **KV 20** *How to analyse the elements of a political speech*):

symbol	an object or sign representing something else	white dove (peace)
metaphor	compares two or more things not using *as*	All the world's a stage. (*Shakespeare*)

Man kann sowohl Symbole wie auch Metaphern leicht übersehen. Ungeübten Lesern wird dies eher passieren als erfahrenen Lesern.
Am Beispiel von *gun* (Objekt der Lebensbedrohung), *tree house* (Ort des Rückzugs und der Beobachtung: Adlerhorst), *jury* (Urteilsmacht eines ganzen Volkes), erarbeiten die SuS im UG, welche symbolische Wirkung von einem Objekt ausgehen kann.

Fragestellung

What is the function of symbols and metaphors in the novel?

Ergebnis

(siehe ausführliche Lösungsskizze **KV 32.2**)
→ Symbols and metaphors add a level of meaning.
→ They can re-inforce the effect of scenes and their message.

Zusatzthema: Kreative Zusatzaufgaben erstellen (1 Stunde)

Hier noch einige kreative Zusatzaufgaben, die jederzeit in der Post Reading-Phase gestellt werden können. Sie runden das Portfolio schön ab. Auch wenn die SuS bereits in einem Alter sind, in dem intellektuelle Beschäftigung dominiert, werden kreative, phantasievolle Aufgaben noch gern übernommen. Sie vertiefen darüber hinaus die deutende Arbeit am Werk.

- Make up Boo's diary by clipping articles and pictures and pasting them in a book. That way, tell the story from his point of view. Use drawings, pictures you cut from a magazine, small objects such as pressed leaves or coins. How does he see the children? How does he see the events? What goes on in his heart?

- Tell the story from Miss Maudie's point of view by writing Miss Maudie's diary.

- Write a monologue made up by individual phone calls Miss Stephanie makes to good friends of hers telling them what goes on in the street and in town. Thus, you may retell the whole story from her point of view.

- Make up a rap in which Lula tells Calpurnia about things after church (cf. **131**). Try and be really cheeky in it. Put it to music and perform it.

- Write a review of the film and hang it up in your classroom.

CLIL-Material: (6 Stunden)

Die folgenden 6 Stundenskizzen sind für den Einsatz von CLIL (*Content and Language Integrated Learning*) im bilingualen Unterricht gedacht. Wenn also im Biologieunterricht, im Gemeinschaftskunde- oder Geschichtsunterricht Querbezüge zu *To Kill a Mockingbird* erwünscht sind, so lassen sich diese Unterrichtsvorschläge einsetzen.

CLIL-Material – Biology (2 Stunden)

Lernziel
Im Roman erwähnte Bezüge zu Flora und Fauna klären.

Methode
Da der Roman zu einer Zeit spielt, die wesentlich weniger technisiert war als das 21. Jahrhundert, haben die beteiligten Personen noch ein sehr enges und selbstverständliches Verhältnis zu Fauna und Flora. Das äußert sich zuerst einmal darin, dass Pflanzen und Tiere mit Namen benannt werden können. Die bloße Namensnennung ruft wiederum dem Leser sofort ein plastisches Bild vor Augen.

Wir schlagen vor, dass die SuS in Arbeitsgruppen kleine Präsentationen der im Roman genannten Tieren und Pflanzen erarbeiten. Photos können wir dazu leider nicht anbieten; sie sind aber im Internet in Hülle und Fülle zu finden. Die Tiere und Pflanzen werden kurz mit englischem und deutschem, eventuell auch lateinischem Namen benannt, beschrieben und im Photo dargestellt. Sodann folgt eine kurze Einordnung, was sie an der jeweiligen Stelle im Roman für eine Funktion haben.

Auf dieser Ebene enthüllt sich neben der Information über die staunenswerten botanischen Alltagskenntnisse jener Zeit eine weitere Dimension des Lee'schen Humors.

Das Arbeitsblatt **KV 33.1/33.2** *Flora and fauna in To Kill a Mockingbird* enthält die notwendigen Informationen.

CLIL-Material – Social studies (2 Stunden)

Lernziel
Rechtsbezüge im Roman erklären.

Methode
Dieses Fachgebiet ist gar nicht so schwierig und entlegen, wie es auf den ersten Blick aussieht. Es eignet sich recht gut zur Integration in den Gemeinschaftskunde- oder Sachunterricht. Bedenkt man, dass juristische Bezüge in unseren Schulcurricula ohnehin unterrepräsentiert sind, so eignet sich eine Doppelstunde zu dem gängigen englischsprachigen Gerichtsvokabular gut, um hier ein gewisses Grundwissen herzustellen.

Der Roman ist reich an Juristenwitzen und gilt in Juristenkreisen aus mehreren Gründen als beste Einführung in ein Jurastudium. Einerseits nimmt er die Paragraphenreiter auf den Arm, andererseits verkörpert er ein System gelebter Gerechtigkeit im Kräftespiel politischer Machtsituationen.

Die Witze vorab. Calpurnia benutzt *Blackstone's Commentaries* als Fibel, um lesen zu lernen. Das wäre etwa so, als würde man einem Erstklässler den Maunz-Düring-Herzog-Grundgesetzkommentar in die Hand drücken, um ihm damit das Lesen beizubringen. Nebenbei – welche Sichtweise auf die geistigen Kapazitäten einer schwarzen Frau drückt Harper Lee damit aus!

Oder: Auf **190** 8 bittet Mr. Gilmer Bob Ewell, *"Would you tell us in your own words what happened on the evening of November twenty-first, please?"* Das kommentiert Scout mit ihrer inneren Stimme: *"Just-in-your-own-words was Mr Gilmer's trade-mark. We often wondered who else's words Mr Gilmer was afraid his witness might employ."*

Einen exzentrischen Sinn für Humor beweist Richter Taylor, als er (**182**) neun (!) Stunden lang dem Verfahren Cunningham gegen Cunningham zuhört und es dann mit dem Verweis auf *"champertous connivance"* – sukzessive Mittäterschaft (d. h. heimliches Einverständnis einer dritten Partei) einstellt.

Der Stundenablauf ist ähnlich wie bei der ersten CLIL-Stunde über Flora und Fauna: die SuS erarbeiten die Terminologie **KV 34.1, 34.2, 34.3** *Legal terminology in To Kill a Mockingbird* in Gruppen und tragen die Begriffe anschließend in einer Präsentation vor. Sie stellen auch jeweils den Bezug zur Textstelle im Roman her.

Zusatzmaterial

CLIL-Material – Historical references in To Kill a Mockingbird (2 Stunden)

Lernziel

Historische Bezüge im Roman klären

Methode

Die historischen Bezüge des Romans haben naturgemäß ihren Platz im Geschichts- oder Gemeinschaftskundeunterricht, wo die Einzelheiten des amerikanischen Bürgerkriegs und der amerikanischen Staatsgeschichte nicht ausführlich beleuchtet werden. Da die daraus resultierenden Spannungen aber bis in die Gegenwart fortwirken, und sei es nur in Form eines latenten Vorurteils des „intellektuellen, aufgeklärten Nordens" gegen den „rassistischen Süden", ist eine Betrachtung der historischen Ereignisse lohnend. Die vorherrschende Sicht des Südens ist noch immer die des Siegers auf den Besiegten, was sich in vielen kleinen Seitenhieben im Roman ausdrückt, etwa wenn Atticus sich über die Belehrungen der „Yankees" und der „distaff side of the Executive branch in Washington" **226** 16 lustig macht.

Folgende Themengebiete, können individuell oder in Gruppen bearbeitet werden:

US History
- Thomas Jefferson, 3rd President **226** 14
- Declaration of Independence **226** 15

The State of Alabama
- history of the State of Alabama
- Alabama Territory **143** 35
- Muskogees (administrative system)
- Governour William Wyott Bibb **143** 37
- Big Mules (in power until 1958)

Slavery
- Missouri Compromise **84** 27

The South
- slavery
- plantation system
- segregation
- Ku Klux Klan
- Jim Crow laws

The Civil War
- Unionist – Confederates
- Yankees **84** 37
- Robert E. Lee (Ewells Vornamen!)
- Brixton Bragg (Underwoods Vornamen)
- CSA pistols **110** 14
- Andrew Jackson, 7th President (Ol' Blue Light **84** 32)
- Brigadier General Wheeler **53** 7

The Great Depression
- The Crash of 1929
- Herbert Hoover, 31st President
- New Deal
- Franklin D. Roosevelt, 32nd President
- poverty in America
- 1935 Work Progress/Project Administration (WPA)
- Dustbowl
- stumphole whisky
- the 1930s

Abschließend sei bemerkt, dass ich diese Form von (PowerPoint-)Vorträgen in meinem Unterricht selbst erprobt habe und sie den Schülern durch die optischen Bezüge die Realität des Romans sehr viel anschaulicher machten.

Zusatzthema: I, Too, Sing America (Langston Hughes) (2 Stunden)

Lernziel

Das Gedicht als Ausdruck wachsenden Selbstbewusstseins der Schwarzen wahrnehmen.

Methode

Im Gegensatz zu den meisten bisher im Unterrichtsmodell besprochenen Texten, präsentiert der Autor in diesem Gedicht einen schwarzen Amerikaner, der hoffnungsvoll ist und sich zutraut sich selbst zu behaupten. Für die SuS wird der Zugang zu dem 1926 – also vor dem Beginn der Romanhandlung – veröffentlichten Gedicht durch die einfache Sprache sowie die klaren Bilder und Metaphern erleichtert. Eventuell bedarf der Begriff *company* der Erläuterung: *a group come together for a social purpose.*

Bevor die SuS den Text selbständig unter verschiedenen Frage- und Aufgabenstellungen bearbeiten

(**KV 35.1**), kann nach dem (Vor-)Lesen des Gedichts zur Einstimmung die Bedeutung des Titels gemeinsam besprochen werden. Direkt fordert der Sprecher hier die Gleichberechtigung ein, nämlich, dass auch er das Recht hat, sich als patriotischer Amerikaner zu verhalten.

Danach kann den SuS jeweils individuell eine der Fragen und Aufgaben der **KV 35.1** zugeordnet werden.

Die *students* A und B sollten ausreichend Gelegenheit haben, ihre Ergebnisse mündlich vorzutragen (im Falle von B auch mit Emphase). Die Arbeitsergebnisse der *students* C, D und E können, eventuell nach einem vorherigen *gallery walk* im Unterrichtsgespräch den anderen zugänglich gemacht werden. Alternativ können deren Ergebnisse vor dem Vortrag der students A und B in einer *placemat*-Runde C, D, E zusammengetragen werden und später dann von Gruppensprechern vorgetragen werden.

Fragestellung
What makes the person in this poem so optimistic?

Ergebnis
(students C)

- contrast: company at the table (in the dining-room) ↔ servants(?) in the kitchen
- eating in the kitchen symbolizes segregation → sent away "when <u>company</u> comes" even though he should be part of the company as a (darker) brother
- speaker is optimistic that he will not be sent away in future, because he will have grown stronger and he will feel self-assured ("beautiful")
- → sitting at the table is symbol of equality

(students D)
optimistic view:

- "laugh", "eat well", "grow strong" → regards black Americans to able to handle their situation
- "tomorrow I'll be at the table" → imagines equality in the near future
- "nobody'll dare", "they'll see", "they'll be ashamed" → counting on white people's understanding and remorse(?)
- → not realistic: equality not achieved; ghettos still exist; aggression of US Police against black Americans continues to this day (Ferguson etc.); …
- → realistic: African-American Civil Rights Movement (Martin Luther King, Malcolm X etc.); black American president; equality achieved in some areas; …

(students E)
images:

- I sing America: → I feel patriotic towards A.
- brother → equal member of the family.
- eat in the kitchen → servant
- laugh, eat, grow strong → positive attitudes to life
- table → place where equals meet

metaphors:

- to be sent to eat in the kitchen → punishment, act of discrimination
- to sit at the table → to be among equals, to be acknowledged

effect of short lines:

- no recognizable rhyme scheme or metre (free-verse poem)
- single words or short lines (run-on lines) stand out more
- → stressed images and metaphors have even greater impact on reader

- → speaker feels self-confident ("strong", "beautiful"), foresees a change of white people's attitudes → because of that optimistic about his future

Zusatzthema: Harlem (Langston Hughes) (2 Stunden)

Lernziel

Die vom Sprecher dargestellten möglichen Reaktionen der Schwarzen auf unerfüllte Träume von Gleichberechtigung darstellen.

Methode

Falls *I Have a Dream* (Modul 6, fakultatives Unterthema) behandelt wurde, können die SuS zum Einstieg daran erinnert werden und gefragt werden, worin der (gesellschaftliche) Traum von Martin Luther King im Jahr 1963 bestand. Ansonsten reicht es aber, an das vorher besprochene Gedicht *I, Too, Sing America* und seinen Optimismus hinsichtlich einer gleichberechtigten Zukunft der Afro-Amerikaner zu erinnern, und zu fragen, wie die dort vorausgesehene Gleichberechtigung wohl im Einzelnen die Situation der Schwarzen verbessern sollte.

Bevor das Gedicht (**KV 35.2**) den SuS ausgehändigt wird, sollte erklärt werden, dass das titelgebende Harlem ein großer, zeitweise prosperierender, zu anderen Zeiten verwahrlosender Stadtteil New Yorks ist. Außerdem ist es für die SuS wichtig zu wissen, dass es

1951 veröffentlicht wurde - 25 Jahre nach *I, Too, Sing America* (und 12 Jahre vor Martin Luther King's *I Have a Dream*).

Danach lesen die SuS das Gedicht und analysieren es mit Hilfe der (**KV 35.3**) zunächst in Einzelarbeit (THINK). Danach ergänzen sie ihren Aufschrieb, indem sie sich mit einem Partner austauschen (PAIR). Dann werden Gruppen mit 4 bis 5 SuS gebildet, die ihre Ergebnisse austauschen (SHARE) und auf ein Blatt der Größe A3 oder besser noch A2 übertragen.

Die SuS sollen danach die Leitfrage beantworten, indem jeder sich begründet für eines der *similes* entscheidet – oder Leistungsstärkere eine eigene Metapher/einen eigenen Vergleich finden.

Es bietet sich an, das Gedicht zum Schluss vortragen zu lassen. Die einzelnen Fragen/Sätze können auch jeweils von einem anderen SoS vorgetragen werden. Der letzte Satz eventuell von allen.

Fragestellung

What do YOU think has happened to the dream that the poem Harlem refers to?

Ergebnis

form → effect

- 4 irregular stanzas: 1 line, 7 lines, 2 lines, 1 line → thoughts are not presented in a regular finished order, but appear spontaneous and indecisive
- 3 end-rhymes: sun-run, meat-sweet, load-explode → the last two are opposites: elements of surprise
- syntax: all sentences but one are questions → vagueness, indecision, helplessness
- climax: last line (like first) stands on its own, asks question, 'violent' verb "explode", stressed by italics → frustration leading to violence

similes → meaning

- dry up like raisin → resignation
- fester like sore/run → painful thought that makes you ill
- stink like rotten meat → something one rejects / doesn't want to come near to
- crust/sugar over like syrupy sweet → something artificial, an illusion, not serious, not necessary
- sags like heavy load → idea/dream that is no longer strong/energetic but weakened and depressing/oppressing

topic – message

- (American) dream of equality/equal civil rights hasn't come true (yet)/(has been "deferred") → disappointment, disillusionment
- the postponed dream turns into something negative/pessimistic (similes); the frustration may turn to violence ("explode") → the unfulfilled (optimistic) dream creates discontent; nobody can say how the people will react

for some the dream may have become

→ smaller until it's no longer there

→ a painful thought/memory

→ an idea one avoids

→ an illusion

→ an idea that has become weak and is no longer valid

→ a dream one has to fight for

→ ...

Harper Lee: *To Kill a Mockingbird*

Portfolio

by _____
(your name)

Kopiervorlage 1 — **Recipe Crackling Bread**

Recipe Crackling Bread

Crackling Bread is mentioned on **32** 04 in the book. Scout loves it. Calpurnia prepares it for her after her first day at school which has been a great disappointment. Anything that could have gone wrong has gone wrong. Crackling Bread is Calpurnia's consolation of Scout.

If you make it for your class, make twice the amount mentioned in the recipe. You should be a somewhat experienced cook to make Crackling Bread.

Crackling bread can best be compared to a French quiche lorraine, except that it has a dry surface. Cracklings are the skin of a pig cut in one-inch squares and rendered (= fried) long enough to leave nothing but the crunchy skin. You may use the grease for cooking and baking. It is best to make your own cracklings. If pig's skin is not available, bacon will do, too. The cracklings should crack when you bite on them, of course.

CRACKLING BREAD
1 egg
1 teaspoon salt
1 teaspoon baking soda
2 cups buttermilk
3 tablespoons flour
1 1/2 cup white corn meal
1 1/2 cups cracklings

add a photo of your crackling bread

How to proceed

Pre-heat oven to 450°.
Make the cracklings and measure them with a cup. If you cannot get hold of pig's skin, you may use 5 slices of bacon. Put 2 tablespoons of the leftover grease into a round 12 inch pan or a 9-inch cast iron skillet. Pre-heat the pan for about 12 minutes.
Mix flour, corn meal, baking soda, and salt in a bowl and add the cracklings. Stir in buttermilk and the beaten egg. Pour batter into the hot pan. Put into hot oven. Bake for 25 – 30 minutes. Serve hot or cold.
You can wrap up your crackling bread and put it on the table at school. It is best cut into 12 or 16 wedges before serving, just like a cake. Each student may take one segment.

Recipe Ambrosia

Ambrosia is mentioned on **91** 01 where it is one of three deserts of Aunt Alexandra's Christmas dinner, along with two kinds of cake. Scout praises her Aunt's cooking and its after-effects: After the meal, the adults sit around in the living-room in a dazed condition. Her brother Jem lies on the floor.
Since you will not serve the full meal, there is no danger of this happening.
Ambrosia literally means "food of the gods". This one is very easy to make. It just takes some shopping and preparing time, so it is best to have 2 or 3 students preparing ambrosia. You don't have to be an experienced cook at all to make it.

INGREDIENTS FOR 12

6 oranges

1 pineapple

1½ cups (sweetened) coconut flakes

a pinch of salt

1 can of spray cream

Add a photo of your own Ambrosia

What to do

Buy the amount of fruit necessary, i. e. two or three times the amount mentioned in the recipe.
Peel the oranges and chop them into ½-inch pieces. This is a somewhat messy business so you may want to wear aprons.
Peel and chop the pineapple into ½-inch pieces. Equally messy. Make sure your fingers are washed well before you start chopping.
In a large china bowl, mix the ingredients and a pinch of salt to intensify the aroma. Cover the top with clingwrap and leave in the refrigerator for at least a day.
That's all.
On the school day, put your ambrosia in an airtight container for transportation. Serve in a nice large bowl (don't forget a spoon). Each student may present his or her little bowl. When it is filled, spray some cream on top.

Recipe Pound Cake

A pound cake is mentioned on **51 18**. Miss Maudie Atkinson gives Scout some to take home after a sad discussion about Boo Radley and Atticus as a lawyer. The pound cake (or poundcake, as it is spelled in the book) is to cheer Scout up. It does.

Some 150 years ago, pound cakes were given this name because the original recipes contained one pound each of butter, sugar, eggs, and flour. Today, the proportions are slightly less rich. Still, it is a cake easy to make. If you are not an experienced cake baker, you should start on this one. It will turn out well if you follow the instructions below.

Take this recipe or look one up on the internet. You may also look for a photo there. Note that there are special measuring cups and measuring spoons in anglo-saxon households. You may want to buy a set on the internet or have one sent to you or buy one during a holiday. They apply in all recipes in the USA, Great Britain, Australia, South Africa, New Zealand, and Canada. They are worth it.

RECIPE

1¾ cups sifted flour

2 teaspoons baking powder

⅛ teaspoon salt

1 cup unsalted butter at room temperature

1 cup castor sugar

4 large eggs, room temperature

2 teaspoons vanilla extract

Zest of a lemon

Note: Instead of castor sugar, you may process 1 cup granulated white sugar in the bowl of your food processor. Process for about 30 seconds.

Add a photo of your own pound cake

What to do

In a large bowl, mix the following dry ingredients: flour, baking powder, and salt.

In another bowl, beat the butter until creamy and smooth. Use a hand mixer or beat it by hand for about 5 minutes and gradually add the sugar while beating continuously on medium high speed. The batter should now be light and fluffy. Add the eggs, one by one, mixing well after each one. Don't worry if the batter looks curdled at this stage. Add the vanilla and lemon zest and keep beating until everything is one smooth batter.

Add the dry ingredients from the other bowl and keep mixing until the batter is even and smooth.

Grease a 9 x 5 x 3 inch loaf pan. Pour batter into pan.

Preheat the oven to 350 degrees. Place the rack in center of oven.

Put the filled pan into pre-heated oven and bake for about 60 minutes until the cake is golden brown and a metal pin pricked into the center comes out clean.

Remove from the oven and place on a wire rack to cool for about 10 minutes. Remove the cake from the pan and let it cool off completely.

Take the poundcake to class in the loaf pan and cut it there on a board. Cut off as many slices as there are students in the class. Don't forget your teacher.

You may eat it with your fingers (or, at home, with a fork).

Presentations   Kopiervorlage 4.1

Presentations

To Kill a Mockingbird is set against the background of the 1930s. Life looked, tasted, felt, and sounded differently then. Television was not invented. People rarely put on the radio. Outdoor and social activities played a larger role than today.
Below you find some expressions and notions from the novel. Find out what they mean and illustrate them with pictures from the internet. Use the material to give a presentation using transparencies or PowerPoint.

Topics for your presentations – 10-20 seconds per picture – one topic per student

A Everyday life objects

- ☐ *4 31* trotline draw (explain that this kind of fishing is not allowed in Germany, and why; and try to make the class guess what kind of character a person would have who resorted to this kind of fishing)
- ☐ *4 37* checker-board (Scout and her father play checkers a lot, and he usually wins)
- ☐ *4 37* hat rack (in every hall there used to be a hat rack)
- ☐ *4 37* spitoon (they disappeared with the smoking of cigarettes; they were to chewing tobacco what butt-ends are to cigarettes, collecting excess mucus in public places)
- ☐ *5 32* Hoover cart (this may be a little hard to find: it is a Tin Lizzie cut in half and drawn by a mule)
- ☐ *5 32* Tin Lizzie (the VW of the 1930s)
- ☐ *5 33* Stiff collar (you can still get them now with formal dress, e. g. tuxedos, but everyone wore them in the 1930s. In the morning, men would just button a new collar to their shirts rather than changing their complete shirts)
- ☐ *8 17* Cowlick (perhaps you have one yourself or someone in class does)

B Curiosities

- ☐ *9 17* picket fence
- ☐ *10 38* stumphole whiskey
- ☐ *11 4* flivver
- ☐ *19 33* union suit, front and rear view
- ☐ *35 23* flagpole sitters (Jem tries to imitate one by spending all day in his tree-house)
- ☐ *36 16* Dunce-cap (the spooky part is that a pupil wearing one looks as if he does not have a head)
- ☐ *36 22* treadmill (try to find a picture with human beings treading one)
- ☐ *38 29* Indian-head (an old coin which the children find as presents)
- ☐ *58 20* Franklin stove (very efficient cast iron stove, invented in 1742)

C Plants

- ☐ *5 33* live oak (a kind of tree that is typical to the south, very big, with a lot of social life under its branches)
- ☐ *8 30* chinaberry tree
- ☐ *9 18* johnson grass
- ☐ *9 19* rabbit-tobacco
- ☐ *9 23* azalea
- ☐ *9 35* pecan tree
- ☐ *12 33* canna
- ☐ *33 9* wistaria (try to find a picture with a large plant making a pretty landscape or garden)
- ☐ *81 8* Bellingrath Garden and House
- ☐ *39 14* camellia (Jem cuts the head off of all the camellias in Mrs Dubose's garden and is punished for it)
- ☐ *56 9* string (Dill constructs a cigarette from it to smoke)
- ☐ *145 22* mandrake roots (a plant which looks like a person and has magical powers)
- ☐ *164 38* Giant Monkey Puzzle (*very* strange looking trees)
- ☐ *189 3* possum (you have to have a look at what ends up in the pots and pans of the black community)

D History

- [ ] Civil War
- [ ] *72 20* battle of Appomattox
- [ ] History of the State of Alabama
- [ ] Robert E. Lee (Confederate General)
- [ ] *47 9* Second Battle of the Marne

E Politics

- [ ] *23 19* The Great Depression ("The Crash")
- [ ] *6 8* Franklin D. Roosevelt ("The only thing we have to fear is fear itself")
- [ ] WAP
- [ ] Prohibition

F Literature

- [ ] Harper Lee
- [ ] Margaret Mitchell: Gone with the Wind (not mentioned in the book but also set in the South during the civil war)
- [ ] *8 36* Victor Appleton: Tom Swift and his motor cycle (a genius inventor whose breakthrough in transport technology form the basis of the plot of the novels)
- [ ] *8 35* Arthur M Winfield: The Rover Boys (The proverbial Tom, Sam and Dick are the original Rover Boys)
- [ ] *17 27* John Singleton Moseby: The Grey Ghost (this is what children devoured at the time)

G Animals

- [ ] *99 35* mockingbird (the emblematic bird – its meaning is explained here)
- [ ] *99 35* bluejay
- [ ] *5 31* mule (a cross between a horse and a donkey, used for transporting virtually everything)
- [ ] *7 9* Rat Terrier (find a gorgeous picture of a puppy)
- [ ] *21 17* hookworm mouth (there is a very drastic photo on the internet)
- [ ] *47 23* pestilence (read about the ten plagues of Egypt and show a picture of a locust pestilence)
- [ ] *181 29* shark and pilot fish (Judge Taylor and his secretary are compared to them, a very funny image)
- [ ] *56 2* Bob-white

H Media

- [ ] *44 36* One Man's Family (a radio series, broadcast from 1932 on)

Religion

- [ ] *49 14* Foot-washing Baptist
- [ ] *49 21* communion

Reading Log

Read *To Kill a Mockingbird* and make notes about the content. Try to re-phrase each chapter in 1-3 sentences. Use this table or copy it into your exercise book.

Reading date	Chapter	Year	Main characters and events in this chapter
	1		
	2		
	3		
	4		
	5		
	6		
	7		
	8		
	9		
	10		
	11		
	12		
	13		
	14		
	15		
	16		
	17		
	18		
	19		
	20		
	21		
	22		
	23		
	24		
	25		
	26		
	27		
	29		
	30		
	31		

Reading Log – Sample Answers

Chapter	Year/Month	Main characters and events in this chapter
Part one		
1	Summer 1933	Description of the Finch family and of Maycomb. Dill arrives. The Radley House is described
2	Early September	Dill leaves. First day of school; Scout meets Walter Cunningham
3		They have lunch with Walter Cunningham. Scout meets the Ewell son. Scout's teacher forbids her to read. Atticus explains to Scout that in order to understand someone else, you have to view things from his or her point of view.
4	Summer 1934	Dill arrives. Scout finds chewing gum in the knothole of the Radley tree. Children start playing the "Boo game"
5		Scout spends a lot of time with Miss Maudie. They want to give Boo a letter. Atticus forbids the "Boo game"
6		They sneak into the Radley property. Jem loses his pants and gets them back coarsely repaired. Dill leaves. They find money in the Radley Tree.
7	Early Nov. 34	Beginning of Scout's second grade. Nathan Radley fills the hole in the Radley tree.
8	November 1934	Mrs Radley dies. Jem and Scout build a snowman. Miss Maudie's house burns down. (At the same time Tom Robinson is arrested, as it turns out later.)
9	December 1934	Atticus accepts the case of Tom Robinson, a black man accused of raping a white woman, Mayella Ewell. Scout is harassed by people, e. g. Cecil Jacobs. Christmas at Aunt Alexandra's: Scout fights with her nephew Francis about Atticus "defending Niggers". Uncle Jack gives Jem and Scout rifles.
10		A mad dog appears and Atticus shoots it. Atticus is a good shot. He tells the children to use their guns wisely: "…it is a sin to kill a mockingbird."
11		Jem's 12th birthday. Jem destroys Mrs Dubose's camellias and has to read to her for punishment. Mrs Dubose dies. The children find out she had fought her morphine addiction to her last day. Scout and Atticus discuss "nigger lovers".
Part two		
12	Summer 1935	Scout notices Jem's adolescence. Dill does not come. Jem and Scout go to Calpurnia's church with her. On returning, Aunt Alexandra has been waiting for them.
13		Aunt Alexandra moves in.
14		Dill turns up unexpectedly in Scout's bedroom
15		Atticus keeps watch in front of Maycomb jail where an angry mob is trying to lynch Tom Robinson in his cell. Scout saves their lives. Dill is allowed to stay.
16	(Trial)	The trial begins. Mr Dolphus is described as an alcoholic.
17	(Trial)	Witness Heck Tate is questioned. Witness Bob Ewell is questioned.
18	(Trial)	Witness Mayella Ewell is questioned.
19	(Trial)	Witness Tom Robinson is interrogated. Atticus gives his final statement. Scout and Jem leave the courtroom because Dill starts crying.
20	(Trial)	Outside, they meet Mr Dolphus and learn that he only pretends to be an alcoholic. He is trying to cover up his excentricity: he has a black wife. The children return to the courtroom and hear the rest of Atticus's speech.
21	(Trial)	Calpurnia appears and takes Jem, Dill, and Scout home. After dinner, they are allowed to return to the courtroom to hear the verdict. At 11 o'clock, the jury announce the verdict: guilty.
22		After the trial, Atticus is spat at and threatened by Bob Ewell.
23		Aunt Alexandra tries to turn Scout into a Southern Lady. Atticus and Jem talk about the law and lawyers. Jem decides that Boo Radly maybe wants to stay at home.
24		Tea party at the Finch house. Aunt Alexandra and her missionary ladies. News of Tom Robinson's death. Dill leaves. Atticus breaks the news to his widow, Helen.
25		Jem is crazy about football. Mr Underwood's editorial about Tom Robinson's death appears in the newspaper.
26	Early September 1935	School starts. Miss Gates, Scout's teacher, tells them about Adolf Hitler, the racist. Scout wonders how someone can be a racist and hate Hitler at the same time.
27	October 1935	Bob Ewell scares Helen Robinson and Judge Taylor. Lin Deas (Helen's boss) successfully tells Bob Ewell to leave. Planning of the Halloween Party.
28	October 31, 1935	Halloween Party. On the way home, Jem and Scout are attacked by Bob Ewell. Ewell is killed by Boo.
29	same night	Scout tells Atticus and Sheriff Tate what happened. She recognizes Boo Radly as her rescuer.
30	same night	Sheriff Tate and Atticus first have an argument about who is responsible for Ewell's death. Tate decides that Bob Ewell fell in his knife in order to spare Boo Radley the publicity of a trial.
31	same night	Scout thanks Boo Radley and escorts him home. Scout and Jem get tucked up in bed by Atticus.

Check yourself questions   Part One

Read *To Kill a Mockingbird* and evaluate the following statements. If the answer is TRUE, tick TRUE, if it is false, tick false and write down the correct answer on a separate sheet.

Is the following statement true or false?	true	false

Part One

1. Scout the narrator remembers the summer that her brother Jem broke his arm. — T F
2. The family live in Maycomb, Alabama. — T F
3. Atticus is the children's father and Calpurnia is their mother. — T F
4. Boo Radley is a grey ghost whom no-one has ever seen. — T F
5. Charles Baker Harris is Dill's official name. — T F
6. Scout is very much looking forward to going to school. — T F
7. Scout can already read before she goes to school. — T F
8. Her first day at school is a great success in every respect. — T F
9. Burris Ewell is one of the best pupils in class. — T F
10. Walter Cunningham does not want to accept lunch money from the teacher. — T F
11. Burris Ewell has lice. — T F
12. After her first day at school, Atticus agrees to Scout being homeschooled. After all, he never went to school either. — T F
13. At the end of Scout's first school year, Dill comes back to spend the summer. — T F
14. The children get really good at dramatizing Boo Radley's life. — T F
15. Atticus admires his children for being such good actors and encourages them to carry on doing so. — T F
16. Scout does not get on very well with Miss Maudie. — T F
17. Miss Maudie is a neighbourhood gossip who talks badly about anybody in Maycomb. — T F
18. Miss Maudie does not like Boo Radley and tells Scout why he is bad. — T F
19. Miss Stephanie Crawford is so lonely that she is glad when Boo Radley comes to her bedroom at night and moves over in her bed. — T F
20. Scout is very bright and understands these allusions to sex. — T F
21. On the last night of Dill's visit, he and Jem are going to sneak up to the Radley porch after dark and peek through a window. — T F
22. Scout decides to go along with Dill and Jem on their most daring game. — T F
23. Jem gets to the porch of the Radley house and can easily peep into the house. — T F
24. Suddenly Boo comes out. — T F
25. The children run for their lives. — T F
26. Dill's trousers get caught in a wire fence. — T F
27. The whole neighbourhood knows within minutes who has shot at an intruder. — T F
28. Jem and Dill have played a game of strip poker. — T F
29. Jem found his trousers torn and crumbled under the fence. — T F
30. The children find a pack of chewing gum and two dolls carved out of soap. — T F
31. Jem suggests writing a thank-you note. — T F
32. Nathan Radley explains to the children that the tree is dying. — T F
33. Jem cries when he figures out the reason why the tree was filled up. — T F
34. That winter, as every winter, snow falls in Maycomb County. — T F
35. Jem finds a way to build a snowman even though there is not really enough snow. — T F
36. Miss Maudie loves plants and does not want them to freeze. — T F
37. Atticus' house burns to the ground. — T F
38. Scout and Jem watch the adults rescue furniture from the burning house. — T F
39. Miss Maudie puts a blanket around Scout's shoulders. — T F
40. Scout has no idea where this blanket came from. — T F
41. Jem decides to return the blanket later. — T F
42. After the fire, the former house-owner is heartbroken. — T F
43. At Christmas, Miss Maudie becomes Uncle Jack's wife. — T F
44. At Christmas, Scout's nephew teases her about Atticus defending a black man. — T F
45. At Christmas, Uncle Jack punishes Scout unjustly. — T F
46. Atticus is nearly fifty years old. — T F
47. Mrs Duboise was a morphine addict. — T F
48. Courage is a man with a gun in his hands. (Definition by Atticus) — T F
49. Tim Johnson dies in the middle of the road. — T F

Check yourself questions Part Two

1. The third summer, Dill does not come to Maycomb. — T F
2. One Sunday, Calpurnia takes the children to First Purchase African M.E. Church. — T F
3. Calpurnia's son Zeebo plays the organ and sings with the congregation. — T F
4. Scout and Jem are treated with great respect by the majority of the congregation. — T F
5. Aunt Alexandra has arrived to live with them. — T F
6. Aunt Alexandra wants Calpurnia to be removed from the house. — T F
7. Scout finds a snake under her bed. — T F
8. Sheriff Tate tells Atticus that his client has been moved to the county jail. There may be trouble. — T F
9. On Sunday night, Atticus tries to protect his client by keeping him company. — T F
10. The children follow Atticus and Scout starts a conversation with Walter Cunningham sj. — T F
11. During the mob scene, a man with a shotgun has Atticus covered the whole time. — T F
12. When the trial is set to begin, Atticus agrees to the children attending it. — T F
13. Blacks and Whites sit in different areas of the courthouse. — T F
14. Dolphus Raymond, a white man, has coloured children. — T F
15. Miss Maudie goes to see the trial along with the other spectators. — T F
16. At the trial, Sheriff Tate has to admit that the woman who was supposed to be raped never underwent medical examination. — T F
17. During cross-examination, Bob Ewell breaks down and admits that Mayella was not raped by Tom Robinson after all. — T F
18. Tom Robinson, the black man, cannot use his right hand due to an accident at work. — T F
19. Tom Robinson feels sorry for Mayella who wanted to kiss him. — T F
20. Dill cries because he cannot bear the ritualised cruelty in Mr Gilmore's way of cross-examining. He feels sorry for Tom Robinson. — T F
21. Dolphus Raymond always sips alcohol from a bottle hidden in a brown paper bag. — T F
22. In his final speech, Atticus implores the white jury to believe the black man's testimony against two white witnesses. — T F
23. Reverend Sykes makes Scout get up in the courtroom because her father passes. — T F
24. Miss Mayella loves flowers and cultivates her own geraniums. — T F
25. After losing Tom Robinson's case, Atticus is despised by the black community. — T F
26. The Missionary Society meets at Miss Maudie's home. — T F
27. Tom's case is won at appeal. — T F
28. Bob Ewell announces his intention to kill someone by saying it made "… one down and about two more to go." — T F
29. Helen Robinson is employed by Link Deas so she can earn money for her family. — T F
30. At the pageant, Scout wears a ham costume which is impossible to get off without help. — T F
31. After the stage performance, Scout and Jem go home together in the dark street. — T T
32. Someone tries to kill the children. — T F
33. The children are defended by an invisible person who kills the attacker. — T F
34. Jem has his right arm broken. — T F
35. Bob Ewell has saved the children. — T F
36. At the end of the novel the children have made Boo come out. — T F

Check yourself questions   Part One – Answers

Part One

1. Scout the narrator remembers the summer that her brother Jem broke his arm. — **T**   F

2. The family live in Maycomb, Alabama. — **T**   F

3. Atticus is the children's father and Calpurnia is their mother. — T   **F**
   Calpurnia is their black housekeeper not their mother. Their mother is dead.

4. Boo Radley is a grey ghost whom no-one has ever seen. — T   **F**
   He is a reclusive neighbour whom no-one has seen in 15 years.

5. Charles Baker Harris is Dill's official name. — **T**   F

6. Scout is very much looking forward to going to school. — **T**   F

7. Scout can already read before she goes to school. — **T**   F

8. Her first day at school is a great success in every respect. — T   **F**
   It is a great disappointment in every respect.

9. Burris Ewell is one of the best pupils in class. — T   **F**
   No, he only ever goes to school on the first day and then plays hooky for the rest of the year.

10. Walter Cunningham does not want to accept lunch money from the teacher. — **T**   F

11. Burris Ewell has lice. — **T**   F

12. After her first day at school, Atticus agrees to Scout being homeschooled. After all, he never went to school either. — T   **F**
    It is true that Atticus was homeschooled but he does not consent to her staying at home.

13. At the end of Scout's first school year, Dill comes back to spend the summer. — **T**   F

14. The children get really good at dramatizing Boo Radley's life. — **T**   F

15. Atticus admires his children for being such good actors and encourages them to carry on doing so. — T   **F**
    He does in fact forbid them to act out Boo's life in the middle of the street.

16. Scout does not get on very well with Miss Maudie. — T   **F**
    She spends a lot more time with Miss Maudie because the boys play in the treehouse on their own.

17. Miss Maudie is a neighbourhood gossip who talks badly about anybody in Maycomb. — T   **F**
    No, that is Miss Stephanie. Miss Maudie lives across the street and is very nice.

18. Miss Maudie does not like Boo Radley and tells Scout why he is bad. — T   **F**
    Wrong. She likes him and tries to make Scout understand him.

19. Miss Stephanie Crawford is so lonely that she is glad when Boo Radley comes to her bedroom at night and moves over in her bed. — T   **F**
    No, that was only a cheeky retort Miss Maudie gave her for being such a gossip.

20. Scout is very bright and understands these allusions to sex. — T   **F**
    No, the incident with Miss Stephanie "moving over in her bed" passes her by completely.

21. On the last night of Dill's visit, he and Jem are going to sneak up to the Radley porch after dark and peek through a window. — **T**   F

22. Scout decides to go along with Dill and Jem on their most daring game. — **T**   F

23. Jem gets to the porch of the Radley house with no difficulty and can easily peep into the house. — T   **F**
    No. Jem, Dill and Scout creep to the porch. They lift Dill, but he cannot look into the window because the curtains are drawn.

Kopiervorlage 6.4   **Check yourself questions   Part One – Answers**

24. Suddenly Boo comes out.   T **F**
 No. A shadow falls on them: Nathan Radley, the elder brother is on the porch.
25. The children run for their lives.   **T** F
26. Dill's trousers get caught in a wire fence.   T **F**
 Jem's trousers get caught in a wire fence.
27. The whole neighbourhood knows within minutes who has shot at an intruder.   **T** F
28. Jem and Dill have played a game of strip poker.   T **F**
 Dill tells Atticus Jem lost his trousers to Dill in a game of strip poker.
29. Jem found his trousers torn and crumpled under the fence.   T **F**
 He found them folded across the fence, mended.
30. The children find a whole pack of chewing gum, two dolls carved out in the garden.   **T** F
31. Jem suggests writing a thank-you note.   **T** F
32. Nathan Radley explains to the children that the tree is dying.   **T** F
33. Jem cries when he figures out the reason why the tree was filled up.   **T** F
34. That winter, as every winter, snow falls in Maycomb County.   T **F**
 It had not snowed in Maycomb County for a hundred years.
35. Jem finds a way to build a snowman even though there is not really enough snow.   **T** F
36. Miss Maudie loves plants and does not want them to freeze.   **T** F
37. Atticus' house burns to the ground.   T **F**
 Miss Maudie's house burns down.
38. Scout and Jem watch the adults rescue furniture from the burning house.   **T** F
39. Miss Maudie puts a blanket around Scout's shoulders.   T **F**
 Boo puts a blanket around Scout's shoulders.
40. Scout has no idea where this blanket came from.   **T** F
41. Jem decides to return the blanket later.   T **F**
 No, he is afraid of Nathan and does not want to return it.
42. After the fire, the former house-owner is heartbroken.   T **F**
 Instead, miraculously, Miss Maudie is in very good spirits. She *is* a stoic.
43. At Christmas, Miss Maudie becomes Uncle Jack's wife.   T **F**
 He does ask her, but only jokingly, on top of his voice, across the street.
44. At Christmas, Scout's nephew teases her about Atticus defending a black man.   **T** F
45. At Christmas, Uncle Jack punishes Scout unjustly.   **T** F
46. Atticus is nearly fifty years old.   **T** F
47. Mrs Duboise was a morphine addict.   **T** F
48. Courage is a man with a gun in his hands. (Definition by Atticus)   T **F**
 Atticus says the opposite. It's when you know you are licked before you begin but you begin anyway and see it through – that's courage.
49. Tim Johnson dies in the middle of the road.   **T** F

Check yourself questions   Part Two – Answers

Kopiervorlage 6.5

1. The third summer, Dill does not come to Maycomb. — **T** F
2. One Sunday, Calpurnia takes the children to First Purchase African M.E. Church. — **T** F
3. Calpurnia's son Zeebo plays the organ and sings with the congregation. — T **F**
   He sings with them but he does not play the organ – there is none. He reads out the hymns and they sing after him. He can read.
4. Scout and Jem are treated with great respect by the majority of the congregation. — **T** F
5. Aunt Alexandra has arrived to live with them. — **T** F
6. Aunt Alexandra wants Calpurnia to be removed from the house. — **T** F
7. Scout finds a snake under her bed. — T **F**
   It is Dill who has run away from home in order to spend the summer with his friends.
8. Sheriff Tate tells Atticus that his client has been moved to the country jail. There may be trouble. — **T** F
9. On Sunday night, Atticus tries to protect his client by keeping him company. — **T** F
10. The children follow Atticus and Scout starts a conversation with Walter Cunninghum sj. — **T** F
11. During the mob scene, a man with a shotgun has Atticus covered the whole time. — **T** F
12. When the trial is set to begin, Atticus agrees to the children attending it. — T **F**
    He asks them to stay away from the courthouse.
13. Blacks and Whites sit in different areas of the courthouse. — **T** F
14. Dolphus Raymond, a white man, has coloured children. — **T** F
15. Miss Maudie goes to see the trial along with the other spectators. — T **F**
    No. "It's morbid", she says. "It's like a Roman carnival."
16. At the trial, Sheriff Tate has to admit that the woman who was supposed to be raped never underwent medical examination. — **T** F
17. During gross-examination, Bob Ewell breaks down and admits that Mayella was not raped by Tom Robinson after all. — T **F**
    He does no such thing.
18. Tom Robinson, the black man, cannot use his right hand due to an accident at work. — T **F**
    He cannot use his left arm. It was caught in a cotton engine.
19. Tom Robinson feels sorry for Mayella who wanted to kiss him. — **T** F
20. Dill cries because he cannot bear the ritualised cruelty in Mr Gilmore's way of cross-examining. He feels sorry for Tom Robinson. — **T** F
21. Dolphus Raymond always sips alcohol from a bottle hidden in a brown paper bag. — T **F**
    The children find out that he really only ever drinks coca-cola but keeps up the appearances of being an alcoholic to explain the eccentricity of his liking to be around black people and having a black woman.
22. In his final speech, Atticus implores the white jury to belive the black man's testimony against two white witnesses. — **T** F
23. Reverend Sykes makes Scout get up in the courtroom because her father passes. — **T** F
24. Miss Mayella loves flowers and cultivates her own geraniums. — **T** F
25. After losing Tom Robinson's case in court, Atticus is despised by the black community. — T **F**
    No, they are grateful and bring lots of food.
26. The Missionary Society meets at Miss Maudie's home. — T **F**
    No, at the Finches.
27. Tom's case is won at appeal. — T **F**
    No, he is shot in prison.
28. Bob Ewell announces his intention to kill someone by saying it made "…one down and about two more to go." — **T** F
29. Helen Robinson is employed by Link Deas so she can earn money for her family. — **T** F
30. At the pageant, Scout wears a ham costume which is impossible to get off without help. — **T** F
31. After the stage performance, Scout and Jem go home together in the dark street. — T **F**
    They don't use the street but a backway through a little wood.
32. Someone tries to kill the children. — **T** F
33. The children are defended by an invisible person who kills the attacker. — **T** F
34. Jem has his right arm broken. — T **F**
    No, his left.
35. Bob Ewell has saved the children. — T **F**
    No, Boo Radley.
36. At the end of the novel the children have made Boo come out. — **T** F

Road Map

The Finch House

Road Map – Solution

Maycomb Tribune
Jail
Tyndal's Hardware Store
Maycomb bank; office

Court-house   The Square

- Post office
- Cecil Jacobs

Maycombe Street in Residential Main

- Miss Henry Lafayette Dubose
- Miss Rachel
- The Finch House
- Miss Maudie Atkinson
- Stephanie Crawford

School | School yard | The Radley House

Group puzzle about chapter 1

Find the answer to your task. Then discuss your answer with the other members of your group and add information you did not have before. – Then change groups. All members of A get together, then all members of groups B. Exchange the information you have about the exposition. Report one by one.

Group 1. Describe the **time** in which the story is set. What year are you in? What does everybody talk about? Describe the economic situation of these years and what it means to people's everyday lives.	A
Group 1. Describe the **time** in which the story is set. What year are you in? What does everybody talk about? Describe the economic situation of these years and what it means to people's everyday lives.	B
Group 1. Describe the **time** in which the story is set. What year are you in? What does everybody talk about? Describe the economic situation of these years and what it means to people's everyday lives.	C
Group 1. Describe the **time** in which the story is set. What year are you in? What does everybody talk about? Describe the economic situation of these years and what it means to people's everyday lives.	D
Group 1. Describe the **time** in which the story is set. What year are you in? What does everybody talk about? Describe the economic situation of these years and what it means to people's everyday lives.	E
Group 2. Read chapter 1 and describe **where** exactly the story is set. Which places are mentioned? Can you identify them on a map? Discuss it with the other members of your group and add extra information.	A
Group 2. Read chapter 1 and describe **where** exactly the story is set. Which places are mentioned? Can you identify them on a map? Discuss it with the other members of your group and add extra information.	B
Group 2. Read chapter 1 and describe **where** exactly the story is set. Which places are mentioned? Can you identify them on a map? Discuss it with the other members of your group and add extra information.	C
Group 2. Read chapter 1 and describe **where** exactly the story is set. Which places are mentioned? Can you identify them on a map? Discuss it with the other members of your group and add extra information.	D
Group 2. Read chapter 1 and describe **where** exactly the story is set. Which places are mentioned? Can you identify them on a map? Discuss it with the other members of your group and add extra information.	E
Group 3. Describe the **history** of the Finch Family, going back as many generations as possible. What happened before the story sets in? What do you know about their social status and their characters?	A
Group 3. Describe the **history** of the Finch Family, going back as many generations as possible. What happened before the story sets in? What do you know about their social status and their characters?	B
Group 3. Describe the **history** of the Finch Family, going back as many generations as possible. What happened before the story sets in? What do you know about their social status and their characters?	C
Group 3. Describe the **history** of the Finch Family, going back as many generations as possible. What happened before the story sets in? What do you know about their social status and their characters?	D
Group 3. Describe the **history** of the Finch Family, going back as many generations as possible. What happened before the story sets in? What do you know about their social status and their characters?	E

Group puzzle about chapter 1

Kopiervorlage 8.2

Group 4. Read chapter 1 and describe the **adult members of the family** you meet. Discuss your results with your group and add information you did not have before.	A
Group 4. Read chapter 1 and describe the **adult members of the family** you meet. Discuss your results with your group and add information you did not have before.	B
Group 4. Read chapter 1 and describe the **adult members of the family** you meet. Discuss your results with your group and add information you did not have before.	C
Group 4. Read chapter 1 and describe the **adult members of the family** you meet. Discuss your results with your group and add information you did not have before.	D
Group 4. Read chapter 1 and describe the **adult members of the family** you meet. Discuss your results with your group and add information you did not have before.	E
Group 5. Describe the **children** in the family. Find out about their character, their sex, and how they get on with one another. Compare your findings with the others in the group. Add what you did not have before.	A
Group 5. Describe the **children** in the family. Find out about their character, their sex, and how they get on with one another. Compare your findings with the others in the group. Add what you did not have before.	B
Group 5. Describe the **children** in the family. Find out about their character, their sex, and how they get on with one another. Compare your findings with the others in the group. Add what you did not have before.	C
Group 5. Describe the **children** in the family. Find out about their character, their sex, and how they get on with one another. Compare your findings with the others in the group. Add what you did not have before.	D
Group 5. Describe the **children** in the family. Find out about their character, their sex, and how they get on with one another. Compare your findings with the others in the group. Add what you did not have before.	E

Characters in chapter 1

Read chapter 1 and make notes about **one** of the following characters:

- ☐ Alexandra's husband
- ☐ Arthur (=Boo) Radley
- ☐ Atticus
- ☐ Calpurnia
- ☐ Jem
- ☐ Miss Stephanie Crawford
- ☐ Mr Radley
- ☐ Scout

His/her name
_____

His/her age _____

His/her best friends
_____

His/her closest relative _____

His/her formal education
_____

He/she makes a living by
_____

He/she lives
_____

His/her biggest problem/secret _____

He/she is afraid of
_____

He/she does not like to talk about
_____

Analysing literary means in chapter 1

Read chapter 1 and make notes about one of the 3 topics below. Where (page/line) do you find examples? Describe their effect (1. Humour; 2. Irritations). Describe their meaning or significance (3. Subplots). One example is given for each topic.

Work on your own on one of the topics for 45 minutes, then compare your results with a partner.

---

1. Humour

3 27 whose piety was exceeded only by his stinginess → sarcasm

2. Irritations

5 13 death of Atticus' first two clients → death as means of punishment

3. Subplots

3 26 – 4 21 Simon Finch's story → sets an example of a successful Alabama family

---

1. _____
2. _____
3. _____
4. _____
5. _____
6. _____
7. _____
8. _____
9. _____
10. _____
11. _____

Understanding Tom's Situation

In 7 different groups, explain how Scout's understanding of Tom's situation changes with each situation described below. Outline her feelings before and after the situation and describe it in a three minute statement in front of the class.

Group 1: Scout is attacked by Cecil Jacobs because her father *defends niggers*. She has a row with him. At Christmas she has a row with her nephew Francis (Chapter 9).

Group 2: Scout eavesdrops on a conversation between Atticus and Jack (Chapter 9).

Group 3: She goes to the black church and understands Helen's situation (Chapter 12).

Group 4: She experiences racial segregation when the mob comes (Chapter 15).

Group 5: She goes to court against Atticus's will and finds seats upstairs in the blacks' gallery (Chapter 16 and Chapter 22).

Group 6: She follows the trial and Atticus's speech (Chapter 20).

Group 7: Miss Gates, Scout's teacher, explains the difference between Nazi Germany and a functioning democracy to the class (Chapter 26).

Strange Fruit

Thomas Shipp and Abram Smith, lynched in Marion, Indiana, on August 7, 1930. Detail of photograph by Lawrence H. Beitler. The photograph that was cited by the songwriter as the inspiration for the song: Thomas Shipp and Abram Smith, August 7, 1930.

Kopiervorlage 12.2 — **Strange Fruit**

All: Watch and listen to Billie Holiday sing that song on
http://www.youtube.com/watch?v=h4ZyuULy9zs

Group 1: Read the lyrics of Billie Holiday's 1939 song and compare it to the picture of the lynched Thomas Shipp and Abram Smith.

Group 2: Try to translate the lyrics into a German poem.

Group 3: Describe the poetic devices of the song. What kind of a rhyme does it use? List the images (e.g. blood on the leaves) and metaphors (e.g. fruit). Comment on the length of words and the contrast in imagery.

Group 4: Read about Billie Holiday's performance of *Strange Fruit* and find out more about the history of the song: http://en.wikipedia.org/wiki/Strange_Fruit .

Group 5: Find out more about lynching in the US: http://www.strangefruit.org/

Strange Fruit

Southern trees bear a strange fruit,
Blood on the leaves and blood at the root,
Black body swinging in the southern breeze,
Strange fruit hanging from the poplar[1] trees.

Pastoral[2] scene of the gallant south,
The bulging[3] eyes and the twisted mouth,
Scent[4] of magnolia sweet and fresh,
And the sudden smell of burning flesh.

Here is a fruit for the crows to pluck,
For the rain to gather, for the wind to suck,
For the sun to rot, for a tree to drop,
Here is a strange and bitter crop[5].

---

1 **poplar** tall straight tree *(Pappel)*
2 **pastoral** relating to farming and countryside
3 **to bulge** to stick out
4 **scent** pleasant smell
5 **crop** plant grown as food; the harvest of this

Is Mr Gilmore a fair prosecutor?

Group A

You are Dill.
During the trial, you observe the way in which Mr Gilmore conducts his cross-examination of Tom Robinson. You (= Dill) put yourself into Tom Robinson's skin. How does Tom feel about everything he hears? Always remember that Tom's life is at stake. One mistake, and he is a dead man. Also remember that a courtroom is there to produce justice. Is Mr Gilmore doing everything to evoke the truth? What effect do his remarks have on the jury? What kind of verdict are they likely to give?

Now read **216** 27–**220** 20 in *To Kill a Mockingbird* again.

Write down everything that you find unjust about Mr Gilmore's way of conducting the interrogation.

Group B

You are Scout.
During the trial, you observe the way in which Mr Gilmore conducts his cross-examination of Tom Robinson. You (Scout) put yourself into Mr Gilmore's skin. What is an attorney's most important task? Remember Mr Gilmore is out there to look at the incident from as many different angles as possible.

Now read **216** 27–**220** 20 in *To Kill a Mockingbird* again.

Write down arguments for Mr Gilmore's way of conducting the interrogation. You do, of course, think him to be fair.

Adventures of Huckleberry Finn – myths and witchcraft   (Expertengruppe 1)

Read the following text. Try to understand as much of the slang and dialect as possible.
Then retell this episode to the others in your group in standard English.

Chapter XXXIV (final passage)

[Huck's good friend, the nigger Jim, has been locked up. Tom Sawyer and Huck Finn assume they know where he is and decide to free him. Tom wants to make it as hard – and adventurous – as possible for them. They rumble around all night considering possibilities to stage a dangerous escape. The next morning they talk to the black man who always brings Jim his food.]

In the morning we was up at break of day, and down to the nigger cabins to pet¹ the dogs and make friends with the nigger that fed Jim – if it WAS Jim that was being fed. The niggers was just getting through breakfast and starting for the fields; and Jim's nigger was piling up a tin pan with bread and meat and things; and whilst the others was leaving, the key come from the house.

This nigger had a good-natured, chuckle-headed face, and his wool² was all tied up in little bunches with thread. That was to keep witches off. He said the witches was pestering him awful these nights, and making him see all kinds of strange things, and hear all kinds of strange words and noises, and he didn't believe he was ever witched so long before in his life. He got so worked up, and got to running on so about his troubles, he forgot all about what he'd been a-going to do. So Tom says:

"What's the vittles³ for? Going to feed the dogs?"

The nigger kind of smiled around gradually over his face, like when you heave a brickbat⁴ in a mud-puddle, and he says:

"Yes, Mars Sid, A dog. Cur'us dog, too. Does you want to go en look at ,im?"

"Yes."

I hunched Tom, and whispers:

"You going, right here in the daybreak? THAT warn't the plan."

"No, it warn't; but it's the plan NOW."

So, drat⁵ him, we went along, but I didn't like it much. When we got in we couldn't hardly see anything, it was so dark; but Jim was there, sure enough, and could see us; and he sings out:

"Why, HUCK! En good LAN'! ain' dat Misto Tom?"

I just knowed how it would be; I just expected it. I didn't know nothing to do; and if I had I couldn't a done it, because that nigger busted in and says:

"Why, de gracious sakes! do he know you genlmen?"

We could see pretty well now. Tom he looked at the nigger, steady and kind of wondering, and says:

"Does WHO know us?"

"Why, dis-yer runaway nigger."

"I don't reckon he does; but what put that into your head?"

"What PUT it dar? Didn' he jis' dis minute sing out like he knowed you?"

Tom says, in a puzzled-up kind of way:

"Well, that's mighty curious. WHO sung out? WHEN did he sing out? WHAT did he sing out?" And turns to me, perfectly ca'm, and says, "Did YOU hear anybody sing out?"

Of course there warn't nothing to be said but the one thing; so I says:

"No; I ain't heard nobody say nothing."

Then he turns to Jim, and looks him over like he never see him before, and says:

"Did you sing out?"

"No, sah," says Jim; "I hain't said nothing, sah."

"Not a word?"

"No, sah, I hain't said a word."

"Did you ever see us before?"

"No, sah; not as I knows on."

So Tom turns to the nigger, which was looking wild and distressed, and says, kind of severe:

"What do you reckon's the matter with you, anyway? What made you think somebody sung out?"

"Oh, it's de dad-blame' witches, sah, en I wisht I was dead, I do. Dey's awluz at it, sah, en dey do mos' kill me, dey sk'yers me so. Please to don't tell nobody ,bout it sah, er ole Mars Silas he'll scole me; ,kase he say dey AIN'T no witches. I jis' wish to goodness he was heah now – DEN what would he say! I jis' bet he couldn' fine no way to git aroun' it DIS time. But it's awluz jis' so; people dat's SOT⁶, stays sot; dey won't look into noth'n'en fine it out f'r deyselves, en when YOU fine it out en tell um 'bout it, dey doan' b'lieve you."

Tom give him a dime, and said we wouldn't tell nobody; and told him to buy some more thread to tie up his wool with; and then looks at Jim, and says:

"I wonder if Uncle Silas is going to hang this nigger. If I was to catch a nigger that was ungrateful enough to run away, I wouldn't give him up, I'd hang him." And whilst the nigger stepped to the door to look at the dime and bite it to see if it was good, he whispers to Jim and says:

"Don't ever let on to know us. And if you hear any digging going on nights, it's us; we're going to set you free."

Jim only had time to grab us by the hand and squeeze it; then the nigger come back, and we said we'd come again some time if the nigger wanted us to; and he said he would, more particular if it was dark, because the witches went for him mostly in the dark, and it was good to have folks around then.

---

1 **to pet** to stroke
2 **his wool** his hair
3 **vittles** *for victuals:* food provisions
4 **brickbat** piece of brick, esp. used as a missile
5 **drat** *swear word*
6 **sot** fool

Myths – find examples in To Kill a Mockingbird (Expertengruppe 2)

To Kill a Mockingbird contains quite a number of myths. They make good stories and are great to tell. In your group, find and list several myths from the novel. The children tell them to each other, and the adults in the community tell some, too.

Give a brief description of the myth/story. Discuss how those myths might have got started and why people might believe them.

page	Myth:
page	Myth:
page	Myth:
page	Myth:
page	Myth:
page	Myth:

Modern Myths (Expertengruppe 3)

You may think the time of urban myths is over since the days of *To Kill a Mockingbird*. Far from it, lots of bizarre modern myths (or urban legends, urban myths) are told today, often re-told over the phone or by email. In many cases, the source can not be provided any more accurately than *FOAF tales*: *Friend of a friend tales*.

Decide which story is the least likely. Retell your story to the others in your group. Do not read it off your notes. Remember you want to see the spark in the other person's eye when you tell your story.

Afterwards explain why you think your story is least likely.

---

❶

A figure is seen in the headlights of a car travelling by night with a single occupant. It is a hitchhiker. The motorist stops and offers the figure a lift. The journey proceeds, after the first minutes in total silence. When the driver stops for the first time at a petrol station one hour later the passenger has vanished. – Tell the story as though it had happened recently to someone you know.

---

❷

It was once a cult among New Yorkers vacationing in Florida to bring back baby alligators for their children to raise as pets. The infant alligators were destined to grow and outlive their cuteness, sad to say, at which point their desperate owners would flush them down the toilet to get rid of them.
Some of these hastily disposed-of creatures survived in the moist Manhattan sewer system and reproduced, the story goes, scattered colonies of full-grown alligators deep below the streets of New York City. Their descendants live down there to this day, hidden from human eyes apart from the occasional impromptu sighting by sewer workers. According to some reports the animals are blind and afflicted with albinism, having lived so long in constant darkness that they have lost their eyesight and the pigment in their skins. Some, they say, have grown to enormous size. – Tell the story as though you heard it as a true story during a recent trip to New York.

---

❸

51-year-old George Turklebaum quietly suffered a fatal heart attack one day while working at his desk. None of his 23 co-workers thought it remarkable to see him slumped motionless in his chair for five days running, apparently, because Turklebaum habitually kept to himself and was the first to arrive and the last to leave the office every day. – Tell the story as though it had happened to a friend of a friend.

---

❹

A man went on a business trip to London. The first night, he met a woman and was seduced by her. The next morning, he woke up in the hotel room minus one kidney. It had been surgically removed for transplantation while he slept and was given anaesthetics. – Tell the story as though it had been on a UK newschannel last weekend.

Racial Segregation

Collect information about everyday life in racial segregation on the internet.

Group 1: Comment on a photo presentation using original black-and-white photographs from the Library of Congress Archives. http://www.loc.gov/rr/print/list/085_disc.html Use overhead transparencies or do a PowerPoint presentation.

Group 2: Give an outline of what segregation means and specify the situation in the United States of America. http://en.wikipedia.org/wiki/Racial_segregation

Group 3: Research the history of former slaves as documented in the Library of Congress. There are several short stories to choose from on this site: http://memory.loc.gov/ammem/snhtml/snvoices00.html
Among them the story of Sarah Frances Shaw Graves, Age 87, a former slave, talking about her parents being alotted to other farmers like chattel:

I was born March 23, 1850 in Kentucky, somewhere near Louisville. I am goin' on 88 years right now. (1937). I was brought to Missouri when I was six months old, along with my mama, who was a slave owned by a man named Shaw, who had allotted her to a man named Jimmie Graves, who came to Missouri to live with his daughter Emily Graves Crowdes. I always lived with Emily Crowdes."

The matter of allotment was confusing to the interviewer and Aunt Sally endeavored to explain.

"Yes'm. Allotted? Yes'm. I'm goin' to explain that," she replied. "You see there was slave traders in those days, jes' like you got horse and mule an' auto traders now. They bought and sold slaves and hired, em out. Yes'm, rented ,em out. Allotted means somethin' like hired out. But the slave never got no wages. That all went to the master. The man they was allotted to paid the master."

"I was never sold. My mama was sold only once, but she was hired out many times. Yes'm when a slave was allotted, somebody made a down payment and gave a mortgage for the rest. A chattel mortgage. . . ."

"Allotments made a lot of grief for the slaves," Aunt Sally asserted. "We left my papa in Kentucky, cause he was allotted to another man. My papa never knew where my mama went, an' my mama never knew where papa went." Aunt Sally paused a moment, then went on bitterly. "They never wanted mama to know, cause they knowed she would never marry so long she knew where he was. Our master wanted her to marry again and raise more children to be slaves. They never wanted mama to know where papa was, an' she never did," sighed Aunt Sally.

Group 4: Read the recorded history of Bones Hooks, a man who nearly got lynched when he was fourteen: Find other reports on http://lcweb2.loc.gov/ammem/ndlpedu/collections/wpa/history.html

Bones, young and inexperienced, had hired out to wrangle horses for a certain cattleman. One day, while he was tending the horses and minding his own business, Vigilantes rode up and asked him, "Are you working for those cattlemen down the creek?" Bones admitted that he was. Before he could says "Jack Robinson", the Vigilantes jerked him up and started to hang him an the nearest tree. They had already hanged the two white men mentioned to other convenient trees....

Bones was certain that they were going to add him to their victims, when Skillety Bill spoke up in behalf of the colored lad, saying that he was a mere boy, wrangling horses for the boss and only carrying out orders of the cattle thief, whom he had taken to be a bona fide cattleman. "A red-haired man astride a limb of the tree gave the rope around my neck a rough jerk", Bones vividly recalled; "and said, Aw, come on, let's got it over with'; but Skillety Bill saved my life."

From the life history: "Texas: [Bones Hooks]," [December 23, 1940]. The interview was conducted as part of a WPA project in the 1930s (United States Work Projects Administration, Federal Writers Project Records).

Group 5: Read the recorded history of Mrs. Mary Thomas telling the story of her father and grandfather who were slaves and escaped slavery, interviewed on October 24 and 25, 1938.

As a child I remember hearing the old folks telling me of their terrible life which they led on the large farms of Maryland before the Emancipation.

My grandfather had been a chieftain's son and he remembered the time when he was a little fellow, playing with some other boys on the banks of the sea, and a band of men swooped down on them and carried them from their own people. My grandfather remembered the heavy gold bracelets and [armlets?] of his rank and those slave-stealers took the gold ornaments from him.

My grandfather had a black mark about an inch wide running down his forehead to the tip of his nose. This mark was the sign of his tribe. He was tall and very much respected by the other slaves and the slave-holder down in Maryland. He married, raised a family and grew old. Even in his old age he was a valuable piece of property, but soon he became useless in the fields and his master agreed to give him his freedom.

But the old man, my grandfather, asked for the freedom of his youngest son, who was my father. This the master refused to do at first but at the earnest insistence of my grandfather, he agreed … upon condition that the son, who was a great swimmer and diver, should dive into the Chesapeake Bay where a ship had sunk years before with a load of iron. If the son were successful in bringing to the surface this load of iron, then my grandfather and his son, my father, should go free.

My grandfather tied a rope around my father's waist and for over three months the two of them brought the pieces of iron to the shore for old master. They say that sometimes the son stayed under the water so long that my grandfather had to drag him up from the wreck and lay him on the {Begin deleted text}[?]{End deleted text} {Begin inserted text}ground{End inserted text} and work over him like you'd work over a drowned person.

Day after day the two worked hard and finally there wasn't no more iron down there and they told the master so and he came down to the wreck and found out they was telling the truth.. but still he wouldn't let them go. The old man, yes, but not the son who was handy around the place, an' everything.

But my grandfather kept asking for his son and the old master said that if the tow of them brought up the sound timbers of the old wreck, then he would keep his word and let them go. So my grandfather and his son, my father, between them brought up all the sound [loose?] timber that was part of the wreck. It was cheaper to get this wood and iron from the wreck than to buy it, so the master wanted it.

The wreck had stayed down on the bottom of the Chesapeake Bay for over twenty years but nobody except my father had been able to dive that deep. So you see it was just like trading off some of the young slaves on the farm to be able to get the iron and wood.

When the two finished that chore, and it was a mighty big chore, too, they went up to the big house and asked for their freedom.

The master sent them back to their cabin and said that since the old man wasn't no good any more, and it just cost the master money to feed him, he could go whenever he pleased, but the son was going to stay on the farm and if he tried any foolishness, he would sell him south. Selling a slave south meant that the slave would be taken to one of the slave trader's jails and put on the block and be sold to some plantation way down south. And no worser thing could happen. Many a family was separated like that, mothers from their children, fathers from their children, wives from their husbands, and the old folks say that a pretty girl fetched (brought) a higher price and didn't have to work in the fields. These young girls, with no one to protect them, were used by their masters and bore children for them. These white masters were the ones who didn't respect our women and all the mixing up today in the south is the result of this power the law gave over our women.

(The old lady was full of horrible examples of the depravity of white masters in the days of slavery. And while I sympathized with her completely, I managed to get her back to the story of her grandfather.)

Well, when the old man and his son knew it was no use, that their master did not intend to let them go, they began to plot an escape. They knew of the Underground Railroad, they knew that if they could get to Baltimore, they would meet friends who would see them to Philadelphia and there the Friends (Quakers) would either let them settle there or send them to other people who would get them safely over the border into Canada.

Well, one night my grandfather and my father made up their minds and my grandfather could read and write so he wrote hisself out a pass. Any slave who went off the farm had to have a pass signed by the master or he would be picked up by a sheriff and put in jail and be whipped.

So my grandfather had this pass and got safely through to Baltimore. There they hid for several days and waited for an agent of the Underground Railroad.

One night they were dressed in some calico [?] homespun like a woman and rode to Philadelphia on the back seat of a wagon loaded with fish. In Philadelphia the town was being searched by slave-holders looking for runaway slaves, so the people where they were supposed to stay in Philadelphia hurried them across the river about ten miles.

(According to the old lady, there were stations of the Underground Railroad all over the East. The Line ran from Baltimore through Wilmington, Delaware, to Philadelphia and there branched off, some of the trails going westward and some leading into New York, with Canada the ultimate goal.)

My grandfather and my father stayed across the Delaware from Philadelphia, helping a farmer harvest his crops, and they built a cabin and soon other escaped slaves from among their former neighbors slipped into New Jersey where they were.

Finally there was almost a hundred escaped slaves in the one spot and because they were free at last and this place was a haven just like the Bible talked about, they decided to stay there and so they got together and called the place Free Haven.

My uncle says that he reached there by hiding in the woods all day and walking at night. So many people came from Maryland that they changed the name of the little village to Snow Hill, which was the name of the town nearest the farms from which all or most of the people had run away from. The post office people made them change the name again and now it is Lawnside, but I was born there sixty-four years ago and I still think of it as Free Haven.

Uncle Toms' Cabin

Harriet Beecher-Stowe (1811-1896) – from her novel Uncle Tom's Cabin (1852)

Retell the story from the point of view of Aunt Hagar, of Mr Haley or Albert.

Chapter XII

About eleven o'clock the next day, a mixed throng[1] was gathered around the court-house steps,—smoking, chewing, spitting, swearing, and conversing, according to their respective tastes and turns,—waiting for the auction to commence. The men and women to be sold sat in a group apart, talking in a low tone to each other. The woman who had been advertised by the name of Hagar was a regular African in feature and figure. She might have been sixty, but was older than that by hard work and disease, was partially blind, and somewhat crippled with rheumatism. By her side stood her only remaining son, Albert, a bright-looking little fellow of fourteen years. The boy was the only survivor of a large family, who had been successively sold away from her to a southern market. The mother held on to him with both her shaking hands, and eyed with intense trepidation[2] every one who walked up to examine him.

"Don't be feard, Aunt Hagar," said the oldest of the men, "I spoke to Mas'r Thomas 'bout it, and he thought he might manage to sell you in a lot both together."

"Dey needn't call me worn out yet," said she, lifting her shaking hands. "I can cook yet, and scrub, and scour[3],—I'm wuth a buying, if I do come cheap;—tell em dat ar,—you tell em," she added, earnestly.

Haley here forced his way into the group, walked up to the old man, pulled his mouth open and looked in, felt of his teeth, made him stand and straighten himself, bend his back, and perform various evolutions to show his muscles; and then passed on to the next, and put him through the same trial. Walking up last to the boy, he felt of his arms, straightened his hands, and looked at his fingers, and made him jump, to show his agility.

"He an't gwine to[4] be sold widout me!" said the old woman, with passionate eagerness; "he and I goes in a lot together; I's rail strong yet, Mas'r and can do heaps o' work,—heaps on it, Mas'r."

"On plantation?" said Haley, with a contemptuous glance. "Likely story!" and, as if satisfied with his examination, he walked out and looked, and stood with his hands in his pocket, his cigar in his mouth, and his hat cocked on one side, ready for action.

"What think of 'em?" said a man who had been following Haley's examination, as if to make up his own mind from it.

"Wal," said Haley, spitting, "I shall put in, I think, for the youngerly ones and the boy."

"They want to sell the boy and the old woman together," said the man.

"Find it a tight pull;—why, she's an old rack o' bones,—not worth her salt."

"You wouldn't then?" said the man.

"Anybody 'd be a fool 't would. She's half blind, crooked with rheumatis, and foolish to boot."

"Some buys up these yer old critturs[5], and ses there's a sight more wear in 'em than a body ,d think," said the man, reflectively.

"No go, 't all," said Haley; "wouldn't take her for a present,—fact,—I've seen, now."

"Wal, t is kinder pity, now, not to buy her with her son,—her heart seems so sot on him,—s'pose they fling her in cheap."

"Them that's got money to spend that ar way, it's all well enough. I shall bid off on that ar boy for a plantation-hand;—wouldn't be bothered with her, no way, not if they'd give her to me," said Haley.

"She'll take on desp't," said the man.

---

1 **throng** crowd
2 **trepidation** fear
3 **to scour** to clean by rubbing its surface
4 **gwine to** going to
5 **critter** creature

"Nat'lly, she will," said the trader, coolly.

The conversation was here interrupted by a busy hum in the audience; and the auctioneer, a short, bustling, important fellow, elbowed his way into the crowd. The old woman drew in her breath, and caught instinctively at her son.

"Keep close to yer mammy, Albert,—close,—dey'll put us up togedder," she said.

"O, mammy, I'm feard they won't," said the boy.

"Dey must, child; I can't live, no ways, if they don't" said the old creature, vehemently.

The stentorian[6] tones of the auctioneer, calling out to clear the way, now announced that the sale was about to commence. A place was cleared, and the bidding began. The different men on the list were soon knocked off at prices which showed a pretty brisk[7] demand in the market; two of them fell to Haley.

"Come, now, young un," said the auctioneer, giving the boy a touch with his hammer, "be up and show your springs, now."

"Put us two up togedder, togedder,—do please, Mas'r," said the old woman, holding fast to her boy.

"Be off," said the man, gruffly[8], pushing her hands away; "you come last. Now, darkey, spring;" and, with the word, he pushed the boy toward the block, while a deep, heavy groan rose behind him. The boy paused, and looked back; but there was no time to stay, and, dashing the tears from his large, bright eyes, he was up in a moment.

His fine figure, alert limbs, and bright face, raised an instant competition, and half a dozen bids simultaneously met the ear of the auctioneer. Anxious, half-frightened, he looked from side to side, as he heard the clatter of contending bids,—now here, now there,—till the hammer fell. Haley had got him. He was pushed from the block toward his new master, but stopped one moment, and looked back, when his poor old mother, trembling in every limb, held out her shaking hands toward him.

"Buy me too, Mas'r, for de dear Lord's sake!—buy me,—I shall die if you don't!"

"You'll die if I do, that's the kink of it," said Haley,—"no!" And he turned on his heel.

The bidding for the poor old creature was summary. The man who had addressed Haley, and who seemed not destitute of compassion[9], bought her for a trifle[10], and the spectators began to disperse.

The poor victims of the sale, who had been brought up in one place together for years, gathered round the despairing old mother, whose agony was pitiful to see.

"Couldn't dey leave me one? Mas'r allers said I should have one,—he did," she repeated over and over, in heart-broken tones.

"Trust in the Lord, Aunt Hagar," said the oldest of the men, sorrowfully.

"What good will it do?" said she, sobbing passionately.

"Mother, mother,—don't! don't!" said the boy. "They say you 's got a good master."

"I don't care,—I don't care. O, Albert! oh, my boy! you 's my last baby. Lord, how ken I?"

"Come, take her off, can't some of ye?" said Haley, dryly; "don't do no good for her to go on that ar way."

The old men of the company, partly by persuasion and partly by force, loosed the poor creature's last despairing hold, and, as they led her off to her new master's wagon, strove to comfort her.

"Now!" said Haley, pushing his three purchases together, and producing a bundle of handcuffs, which he proceeded to put on their wrists; and fastening each handcuff to a long chain, he drove them before him to the jail.

---

6 **stentorian** loud
7 **brisk** strong
8 **gruffly** unfriendly and impatiently
9 **not destitute of compassion** not lacking sympathy
10 **trifle** negligible sum

Steps in the Civil Rights Movement

Prepare a 5-minute presentation on one of the following subjects. You may also search YouTube for some short videos.

Group 1: The Scottsboro Trials – 1931. Nine blacks were accused of raping and killing two white women on a train and never got a fair trial.
http://en.wikipedia.org/wiki/Scottsboro_Boys

Group 2: Rosa Parks and the Montgomery Bus Boycott – 1955
http://www.watson.org/~lisa/blackhistory/civilrights-55-65/montbus.html

Group 3: Martin Luther King's speech in Washington "I have a dream" – 1963 claiming Equal Rights granted in the American Constitution (non violent actions).
http://www.americanrhetoric.com/speeches/mlkihaveadream.htm

Group 4: Civil Rights Act of 1964 – which prohibited racial discrimination in hiring practices and public services in the United States.
http://en.wikipedia.org/wiki/Civil_Rights_Act_of_1964

Group 5: Malcom X – 1965 (violent actions)
http://en.wikipedia.org/wiki/Malcolm_X

Group 6: A Bridge in Selma – 1965 – 600 Blacks got beaten up on their march to Montgomery, Alabama, in order to be entered into the voters' lists.
http://en.wikipedia.org/wiki/Selma_to_Montgomery_marches

Group 7: The first Black American President.
http://www.whitehouse.gov/administration/president_obama/

How to analyse the elements of a political speech

I. Rhetorical devices

Find other examples for the different rhetorical devices given in the list.

name	definition	example
allegory	a figure of speech conveying a meaning other than the literal.	rose (= *love*)
alliteration	the repetition of the first consonant sound in a phrase	Peter Piper picked a peck of pickled peppers
anaphora [əˈnæfərə]	repetition of a word or phrase at the beginning of sucessive clauses	There was .../ There was .../ There was ...
antithesis [ænˈtɪθəsɪs]	opposites	the rich and the poor
chiasmus [kaɪˈæsməs]	an inversion of the relationship between four elements of phrases, representing the Greek letter chi (χ)	To stop too fearful, and too faint to go.
climax	a string of words or clauses - usually three - in rising order of forcefulness	not just for our nation, not only for all humanity, but for life upon the earth
ellipsis [ɪˈlɪpsɪs]	omitting a word while the sentence can still be understood	How many people were present? – Thirty-five (people).
euphemism [ˈjuːfəmɪzəm]	a paraphrase expressing something brutal or hard by something gentle or easy to accept	pass away (instead of die)
exclamation	emphatic expression	Oh dear! Oh joy! Great!
inversion	changing the usual grammatical order of words	his hand dropt he
irony	saying the opposite of what is meant	they did a great job (their work was bad)
litotes [laɪˈtəʊtiːz]	negation of the opposite (way of understatement to emphasise a statement)	I was not a little upset
metaphor	compares two or more things not using *as*	All the world's a stage. (Shakespeare)
onomatopoeia [ɒnəmætəˈpiːə]	words that imitate their meanings by the sounds that they make	to whisper, to boo
parallel structure	repetition of word sequence	We have come so far. We have seen so much.
personification	inanimate objects or things are endowed with human qualities	the tree was sad
rhetorical question	the speaker does not really expect an answer from the audience but wants to awake their attention	And who could object to such an offer?
simile [ˈsɪməliː]	used to compare two things, usually with the words *like* or *as*	(as) white as snow
symbol	an object or sign representing something else	white dove (peace)
tautology [tɔːˈtɒlədʒi]	unnecessary use of two words with the same meaning	an unmarried bachelor

II. Structure of a speech

Introduction	The speaker tries to get his audience's attention. – How does the speaker achieve this? – How does he address his audience? – How does he define himself in relation to the audience?
Statement of the present situation	The speaker characterizes the present situation from his point of view. – How are things now? – How were they before? – How have we come so far? – What kind of development has taken place?
Reasoning	The speaker argues his main point. – What has he come here for? – What is the cause of his campaign? In confrontation with different opinions his own one is to appear as the superior one.
Peroration / Final phrase	The end of the speech culminates in a short command or appeal as how to proceed from here.

Tip
- In order to analyse a speech, discern the elements of **structure** first.
- Then sum up the **main argument** of the speech in a few sentences.
- Then list some of the **rhetorical devices** the speaker employs and comment on their effect.

The Gettysburg Address

On November 19th, 1863, President Abraham Lincoln made the following two-minute speech at the opening of Gettysburg Cemetery in front of an audience of 150,000. Four and a half months ago, 40,000 soldiers had lost their lives there on the largest battlefield of the American Civil War (1861-1865). His speech, one of the most famous in American history, has been remembered as *Gettysburg Address*. It is part of the American heritage, and all American school children have to learn it by heart. It is considered a rhetorical masterpiece since Lincoln outlines in very few words the reason of the conflict between Unionists and Confederate States. His closing phrase *government of the people, by the people, for the people* sums up America's democratic concept.

Read the speech and comment on its structure and rhetorical devices.

> Four score[1] and seven years ago our fathers brought forth[2], upon this continent, a new nation, conceived in Liberty, and dedicated to the proposition that all men are created equal.
>
> Now we are engaged in a great civil war, testing whether that nation, or any nation, so conceived, and so dedicated, can long endure[3]. We are met here on a great battlefield of that war. We have come to dedicate a portion of it as a final resting place for those who here gave their lives that that nation might live. It is altogether fitting and proper that we should do this.
>
> But in a larger sense we can not dedicate – we can not consecrate[4] – we can not hallow[5] this ground. The brave men, living and dead, who struggled, here, have consecrated it far above our poor power to add or detract. The world will little note, nor long remember, what we say here, but can never forget what they did here. It is for us, the living, rather to be dedicated here to the unfinished work which they have, thus far, so nobly carried on. It is rather for us to be here dedicated to the great task remaining before us – that from these honored dead we take increased devotion to that cause for which they here gave the last full measure of devotion – that we here highly resolve that these dead shall not have died in vain; that this nation shall have a new birth of freedom; and that this government of the people, by the people, for the people, shall not perish[6] from the earth.

---

1 **four score** four times twenty
2 **to bring forth** to give birth to
3 **to endure** to suffer, to continue to exist
4 **to consecrate** to state officially that sth is holy
5 **to hallow** to make holy
6 **to perish** to be lost, to die

I have a dream

I am happy to join with you today in what will go down in history as the greatest demonstration for freedom in the history of our nation.
Five score years ago, a great American, in whose symbolic shadow we stand today, signed the Emancipation Proclamation. This momentous decree came as a great beacon light of hope to millions of Negro slaves who had been seared in the flames of withering injustice. It came as a joyous daybreak to end the long night of their captivity.

But one hundred years later, the Negro still is not free. One hundred years later, the life of the Negro is still sadly crippled by the manacles of segregation and the chains of discrimination. One hundred years later, the Negro lives on a lonely island of poverty in the midst of a vast ocean of material prosperity. One hundred years later, the Negro is still languishing in the corners of American society and finds himself an exile in his own land. So we have come here today to dramatize a shameful condition.
In a sense we have come to our nation's capital to cash a check. When the architects of our republic wrote the magnificent words of the Constitution and the Declaration of Independence, they were signing a promissory note to which every American was to fall heir. This note was a promise that all men, yes, black men as well as white men, would be guaranteed the unalienable rights of life, liberty, and the pursuit of happiness.

It is obvious today that America has defaulted on this promissory note insofar as her citizens of color are concerned. Instead of honoring this sacred obligation, America has given the Negro people a bad check, a check which has come back marked "insufficient funds." But we refuse to believe that the bank of justice is bankrupt. We refuse to believe that there are insufficient funds in the great vaults of opportunity of this nation. So we have come to cash this check — a check that will give us upon demand the riches of freedom and the security of justice. We have also come to this hallowed spot to remind America of the fierce urgency of now. This is no time to engage in the luxury of cooling off or to take the tranquilizing drug of gradualism. Now is the time to make real the promises of democracy. Now is the time to rise from the dark and desolate valley of segregation to the sunlit path of racial justice. Now is the time to lift our nation from the quick sands of racial injustice to the solid rock of brotherhood. Now is the time to make justice a reality for all of God's children.

There will be neither rest nor tranquility in America until the Negro is granted his citizenship rights. The whirlwinds of revolt will continue to shake the foundations of our nation until the bright day of justice emerges.

But there is something that I must say to my people who stand on the warm threshold which leads into the palace of justice. In the process of gaining our rightful place we must not be guilty of wrongful deeds. Let us not seek to satisfy our thirst for freedom by drinking from the cup of bitterness and hatred. We must forever conduct our struggle on the high plane of dignity and discipline. We must not allow our creative protest to degenerate into physical violence. Again and again we must rise to the majestic heights of meeting physical force with soul force.

The marvelous new militancy which has engulfed the Negro community must not lead us to a distrust of all white people, for many of our white brothers, as evidenced by their presence here today, have come to realize that their destiny is tied up with our destiny. They have come to realize that their freedom is inextricably bound to our freedom. We cannot walk alone.

As we walk, we must make the pledge that we shall always march ahead. We cannot turn back. There are those who are asking the devotees of civil rights, "When will you be satisfied?" We can never be satisfied as long as the Negro is the victim of the unspeakable horrors of police brutality. We can never be satisfied, as long as our bodies, heavy with the fatigue of travel, cannot gain lodging in the motels of the highways and the hotels of the cities. We can never be satisfied as long as our children are robbed of their dignity by signs stating "For Whites Only". No, no, we are not satisfied, and we will not be satisfied until justice rolls down like waters and righteousness like a mighty stream.

I have a dream

I am not unmindful that some of you have come here out of great trials and tribulations. Some of you have come fresh from narrow jail cells.

Go back to Mississippi, go back to Alabama, go back to South Carolina, go back to Georgia, go back to Louisiana, go back to the slums and ghettos of our northern cities, knowing that somehow this situation can and will be changed. Let us not wallow in the valley of despair.

I say to you today, my friends, so even though we face the difficulties of today and tomorrow, I still have a dream. It is a dream deeply rooted in the American dream.
I have a dream that one day this nation will rise up and live out the true meaning of its creed: "We hold these truths to be self-evident: that all men are created equal."
I have a dream that one day on the red hills of Georgia the sons of former slaves and the sons of former slave owners will be able to sit down together at the table of brotherhood.

I have a dream that one day even the state of Mississippi, a state sweltering with the heat of injustice, sweltering with the heat of oppression, will be transformed into an oasis of freedom and justice.

I have a dream that my four little children will one day live in a nation where they will not be judged by the color of their skin but by the content of their character.
I have a dream today.

I have a dream that one day, down in Alabama, with its vicious racists, with its governor having his lips dripping with the words of interposition and nullification; one day right there in Alabama, little black boys and black girls will be able to join hands with little white boys and white girls as sisters and brothers.

I have a dream today.

I have a dream that one day every valley shall be exalted, every hill and mountain shall be made low, the rough places will be made plain, and the crooked places will be made straight, and the glory of the Lord shall be revealed, and all flesh shall see it together.

This is our hope. This is the faith that I go back to the South with. With this faith we will be able to hew out of the mountain of despair a stone of hope. With this faith we will be able to transform the jangling discords of our nation into a beautiful symphony of brotherhood. With this faith we will be able to work together, to pray together, to struggle together, to go to jail together, to stand up for freedom together, knowing that we will be free one day.

This will be the day when all of God's children will be able to sing with a new meaning, "My country, ,tis of thee, sweet land of liberty, of thee I sing. Land where my fathers died, land of the pilgrim's pride, from every mountainside, let freedom ring."
And if America is to be a great nation this must become true.

So let freedom ring from the prodigious hilltops of New Hampshire!
Let freedom ring from the mighty mountains of New York!
Let freedom ring from the heightening Alleghenies of Pennsylvania!
Let freedom ring from the snowcapped Rockies of Colorado!
Let freedom ring from every hill and molehill of Mississippi. From every mountainside, let freedom ring.

And when this happens, when we allow freedom to ring, when we let it ring from every village and every hamlet, from every state and every city, we will be able to speed up that day when all of God's children, black men and white men, Jews and Gentiles, Protestants and Catholics, will be able to join hands and sing in the words of the old Negro spiritual, "Free at last! free at last! thank God Almighty, we are free at last!"

Atticus' personality traits

Characterising Atticus

What kind of person is Atticus? Is he cold and inaccessible? Or is he full of warm sympathy for the underprivileged? Does he know how to treat children or does he only let them run wild? Does he have a fair feeling of justice or is he a dreamer much like *Kleist's Michael Kohlhaas*?
How do the different characters in the book see him? Work in groups first. Assess the arguments each character would come up with. Then try and promote your view of his character in a panel discussion.

Group 1
How does his sister Alexandra see him, particularly in chapter 14?

Group 2
How does Jem see Atticus?

Group 3
How would Scout describe Atticus?

Group 4
How would Mr Underwood describe Atticus? (see pp 170/171; 265/266)

Group 5
How would Judge Taylor describe Atticus?

Group 6
What kind of person is Atticus according to Mayella Ewell?

Group 7
What kind of characterization would Mr Cunningham give?

Eulogy on Atticus

Eulogy [ˈjuːlədʒɪ] on Atticus

In English-speaking countries, it is customary to praise people on special occasions in a special way. One refers to their character and their work in a humorous and intimate way and somehow explains to everybody around what a wonderful person the praised one is. You follow certain rules which are not usually laid down in writing:

Structure of a eulogy
1. Make a joke.
2. Then talk about one event in his life as an anecdote.
3. Summarize his three greatest qualities.
4. End your eulogy on one witty or praising word and a toast.

On the occasion of Atticus's 60th birthday, you are to make a short speech in his honor. Develop the elements of your personal eulogy in the followinig steps.

First, collect those qualities that are characteristic of him.

_____
_____
_____
_____
_____
_____
_____
_____
_____
_____

Then, select the one you will talk about in detail. Use one of the events described in the book and re-tell it as an anecdote.

_____

Then, think of a joke as an introduction to your speech

_____
_____
_____

Think of who else is going to be there. Do you need to address them? How?

_____

Now write down your complete speech.

_____
_____
_____
_____
_____
_____
_____

Role models for southern ladies

Cover Illustration taken from the cover of Harper's Weekly, September 7, 1861 showing a typical "Southern Belle"

The idea of a Southern Belle ("Beauty of the Southern States") signifies the stereotype of a young, refined and sophisticated beautiful white woman from the American South.

A *Southern Belle* was born and raised in the upper class and has relished extensive instruction. She appears proud and self-confident. She knows how to make polite conversation and enjoys welcoming guests. She knows how to present herself in the most beautiful clothes, and her chief occupation is being herself. Being the equivalent of a "höhere Tochter" in the German speaking countries, the *Southern Belle* has the added quality of *Southern charme and fire*. It is not atypical for a *Southern Belle* to show some snobbish class conceit and look down upon the less well off classes. She may even be a prim and affected, uppity woman trying with all her might to preserve youth and beauty.

The concept of *Southern Belle* was coined after the defeat of the Confederate Army in the American Civil War and is part of the myth of the Lost Cause and the *good ol' times* before the war. The most prominent *Southern Belle* in American literary history is Scarlett O'Hara, protagonist in Margaret Mitchell's Novel *Gone with the Wind*.

Stages of Scout's sexual identity

Group 1 – Summer 1933

- Analyse her relationship with Jem and Dill. Define her sexual identity in relation to them. Is it similar or different?
- Analyse her relationship with Calpurnia. How could you define the role relationship between them? Do they get on with one another? How does Calpurnia want Scout to behave? What kind of sexual identity does Calpurnia expect from Scout?
- Analyse the way Scout's mother lives on within her. How does she feel about her mother? Does her mother's image live on within Scout? Does she identify with her mother? What do you imagine Scout's mother was like?

Group 2 – Summer 1934

- Analyse her relationship with Jem and Dill. Define her sexual identity in relation to them. Is it similar or different? Does Scout agree with the boys' judgement?
- Analyse her relationship with Miss Maudie. What do they do together? What does Scout admire in Miss Maudie? Does Miss Maudie have a more feminine or a more masculine personality? To what extent does Miss Maudie influence Scout's sexual identity?
- Analyse the difference between Miss Maudie's and Calpurnia's influence on Scout's identity. Is their influence similar, identical or different? How feminine do you rate the three women?

Group 3 – Summer 1935

- What does Scout suddenly realize regarding Calpurnia and Zeebo? Analyse if these new findings influence Scout's feelings towards Calpurnia. Do they have any consequences regarding Scout's sexual identity?
- Aunt Alexandra, too, notices something about Scout, Calpurnia and Zeebo. Analyse what it is and how she reacts to it.
- Analyse the kind of sexual identity that Aunt Alexandra tries to instil within Scout. How successful is she?

Group 4 - Summer 1935

- Compare the father-daughter-relationship between Mayella Ewell and her father and Scout and her father.
- Compare the mother-daughter-situation between Mayella Ewell and her mother and Scout and her mother.
- Scout is engaged to Dill. Mayella Ewell desires a sexual relationship with Tom Robinson. Compare their sexual identities.
- Analyse Scout's view of Mayella Ewell in terms of her own sexual development.

Group 5 – October 31, 1935

- Analyse the meaning of the overalls for Scout's sexual identity in general.
- How do you interpret the fact that Aunt Alexandra puts Scout's overalls on after Bob Ewell has got killed?
- Think of the final image of Boo and Scout sitting on the swing together on the Finch porch. How can you interpret this in terms of both Scout's and Boo's sexual identity?
- Give a final judgement on Scout's interpretation of women. Does she want to be a woman like the women around her? Analyse Scout's sexual identity at the end of the book.

Viewing Log

Group 1

While you watch the film *To Kill a Mockingbird*, please make notes about the following:

1. Which parts of the book were shortened?
2. Which scenes from the book did you miss?
3. Was the dialogue close to the novel or loosely based on the novel?

Group 2

While you watch the film *To Kill a Mockingbird*, please make notes about the following:

4. Did you imagine Scout to look the way she did? Was she well cast?
5. Is Grerory Peck convincing as Atticus? Which is your favourite scene? Why?
6. Did you imagine Boo to look and act that way? What do you think of his acting?
7. Who is your favourite actress / actor in the film?

Group 3

While you watch the film *To Kill a Mockingbird*, please make notes about the following:

8. Compare the set to the pictures of Monroeville you have seen on the internet. How do you like the set?
9. How does the film balance sentiment and intellect?
10. Which is your favourite scene?

Group 4

While you watch the film *To Kill a Mockingbird*, please make notes about the following:

11. What did you not like about the movie?
12. What is the effect of the music?
13. Compare the effect of 30 hours reading the book and 129 minutes watching the movie. Which of the two left a deeper impression on you? In which way were they different?

Topics for a panel discussion

Choose a topic that you are interested in, then find 2 or 3 people who are interested in the same subject. Take 5 minutes to individually prepare your arguments. Then exchange your arguments in front of the class.

Topic 1: Is growing up today still similar to the times of Scout and Jem?
Topic 2: Has the role of women in society really changed that much since 1935?
Topic 3: Injustice in court – is that still a subject today?
Topic 4: Atticus – a model father?
Topic 5: Are good and evil portrayed realistically in *To Kill a Mockingbird*?
Topic 6: Dracula and The Grey Ghost – who has taken their place in today's media?
Topic 7: What I disliked about the book.
Topic 8: What I liked most about the book.
Topic 9: Have I learned something from the book?

My subject _____

My arguments _____

_____

_____

_____

_____

_____

_____

_____

_____

_____

_____

_____

_____

Friday, September 14, 2007

Harper Lee's novel is a racist morality tale

By FRED LEEBRON
SPECIAL TO THE P-I (Seattle Post Intelligencer)

As your typical left-leaning liberal in need of a vacation from the redneck celebration of life in these United States, I ought to be glad that "To Kill a Mockingbird" endures like Styrofoam in this country. I'm happy for Harper Lee that her one novel was a rock-solid, best-selling, completely accessible to one and all morality tale. The problem, as I see it, with all this practiced obsession with "Mockingbird" is that, on second and third glance, it clearly does not treat its black "folk" as equally complex and subtle as the full spectrum of white "folk" in Maycomb; it does not step back and allow these downtrodden blacks free rein in the same vein it allows its whites. It does not even allow them the same capacity for elastic speech as it allows its 8-year-old protagonist, Scout. In Mockingbird, the black folk are as simple-spoken as toast, and they're ever so lucky to have Atticus Finch on their side. I mean, isn't it grand that Tom Robinson, the black guy who had the misfortune to come into contact with the white girl (and who dared to rebuff her advances and who dared to testify that he felt sorry for her) is killed by relatively faceless white law-enforcement officials, even though Tom is as innocent of the accusation of rape as Snow White? And isn't it grander still that Mr. Ewell, father of the white girl and the actual false accuser here, is murdered by Boo Radley, a mysterious faceless character right out of Huck Finn (see: Injun Joe), while we all learn the hard lesson that we can't ever know the true essence of any person without walking in his or her shoes?

Let's face it, in some facets, "Mockingbird" is a transparently bigoted work. "It occurred to me," Scout tells us as she witnesses Tom Robinson's testimony at the trial, "that in their own way, Tom Robinson's manners were as good as Atticus's." In their own way? Is it only me, or isn't it disturbing how readily accepting we all are of an 8-year-old's assessment of a full-grown black man's behavior? That Scout's voice is somehow supposed to be the voice of wisdom?

While "To Kill a Mockingbird" would like to teach us that racism is skin deep, what it ultimately teaches us is that we will never fully understand the truth about race relations in this country. Perhaps white readers derive a secret thrill (or at least experience a private sense of affirmation) at the limited intelligence of its black characters and at the nefarious outcome of its black protagonist. After all, the black victim not only declined a white girl's advances -- he also was shot attempting to escape the white man's jail, so it must be OK that he was brought down by 17 bullets from faceless white guards ("He wasn't Tom to them," Atticus says, "he was an escaping prisoner"). As Harper Lee notes in the introduction to the 35th anniversary edition of the novel, "Mockingbird still says what it has to say." I'm afraid it does.

I wish I could say I was mystified by the continued act of literary obeisance we pay this clearly limited and exaggerated tale, a book that could just as well be read as a young-adult novel, but why should I be? In this age of an ever-dwindling white majority, we continue to profess our transcendence of racism when it is all we ever practice.

Fred Leebron is a novelist whose works include "Six Figures" and "In The Middle of All This." He co-edited "Postmodern American Fiction: A Norton Anthology."

Walk and Swap – Leebron's Arguments

Write one of Lebron's arguments here. On the back, add your own opinion about that point.	*Write one of Lebron's arguments here. On the back, add your own opinion about that point.*
Write one of Lebron's arguments here. On the back, add your own opinion about that point.	*Write one of Lebron's arguments here. On the back, add your own opinion about that point.*

What's in a name?

Find literary associations, philosophical and historical allusions, phonetic and metaphorical allusions.

name	task	your results
Atticus	– Research "Attica" and "Attic philosophy". Where is it situated? Which large town is situated there? – Look up meanings of "Attic".	
Boo	– Find out what English-speaking parents mean when they say "peekaboo" or "peek-a-boo" to their one-year-old children.	
Calpurnia	– Find out who Calpurnia was in relation to Julius Caesar. – Point out any resemblance in relation to Calpurnia and her employer.	
J. Grimes Everett	– Find a related adjective to his first name.	
Jeremy	– Describe the vocation its first bearer had.	
Merriweather, Grace	– Give a literal translation of the name. – Determine if the name is an exact description or the opposite of her character. – Which pun is made with her first name?	
Mockingbird	– Name the most distinctive features of a mockingbird. (Don't be confused by the German translation – it is misleading.) – Which two characters in the book are metaphorically called "mockingbirds"? – Do you think they fit the meaning of the name?	
Mrunas	– Give a characterization of the phonetic quality of the name (onomatopoeia). – What kind of correspondence between sound and supposed traits can you detect?	
Scout	– What could be the metaphorical meaning of the name?	
Tom Robinson	– Which other famous black American do you know in the literary world that bears the same first name? – Which other famous person do you know in literature that bears the same second name? – Find a relation between Tom Robinson and Tim Johnson – in which regard do they resemble each other? – What's the meaning of the expression "… before he could say *Jack Robinson* …".	
Underwood	– Give a literal translation of the name. – Find out if the name describes the intentions of its bearer.	

What's in a name?

name	possible results
Atticus	– Attica – region in Greece with capital Athens. Attic philosophy. – Attic is synonymous with the adjectives "classical", "simple", "restrained". – "Attic faith" means "unshakable faith", "Attic wit" means "graceful or piercing wit".
Boo	– Children hide and when adults cry "boo" they pretend to be frightened.
Calpurnia	– She was the last wife of Julius Caesar and stood in opposition to Cleopatra when she came to Rome. – The night before Caesar's death she dreamt he was killed and implored him not to leave the house, but he did and was murdered. (→ Blacks liked to give their children Roman names.)
J. Grimes Everett	– The missionary is "grimy", dirty in his heart when he goes to reform the Mrunas.
Jeremy (Jem)	– Jeremy was a Jewish prophet.
Merriweather, Grace	– *Frau Fröhlichwetter* knows her place in society: she introduces the missionary. She is on the bright side of life. She is a 'good woman'. – "Amazing Grace" is sung with gentle mockery by her husband. – Mrs Merriweather's name is cutting satire on the part of Harper Lee, for although she pretends to worry about the black Mrunas she has no respect for the black people in her own community. Her attitude is condescending.
Mockingbird	– Sings no song of its own, mimicks the songs of insect and amphibian sounds as well as other bird songs, often loudly and in rapid succession. Has no function in life but to sing its heart out. – Tom Robinson and Arthur Radley. – Neither has done any harm to others.
Mrunas	– Their (made up) name sounds dirty, consonantal, wild and threatening and fulfils every cliché a white American has about black Africans. – The Mrunas are also called a "primitive" African tribe which believes that a child doesn't have one father or one mother, but rather, as many fathers and mothers as there are men and women in the community. (Scout and Jem, too, have Calpurnia, Aunt Alexandra, Miss Maudie and Boo as extra fathers and mothers in their community).
Scout	– A Scout, who finds her own way in life in the *Bildungsroman*.
Tom Robinson	– Uncle Tom of "Uncle Tom's Cabin". – Robinson Crusoe, who had to re-invent civilization on his lonely island. → Atticus says that Tom wasn't an *"Old Uncle"* (225 9). → Tom Robinson is an *Uncle Tom* of the 20th century. – Tim Johnson is the mad dog that is shot by Atticus. Tim the mad dog and Tom the underdog are both innocent and both get shot. – The English expression "before he could say Jack Robinson" means that something happens very quickly. → "Before he could say Jack Robinson, Tom Robinson was a dead man".
Underwood	– *Unterholz* – A hidden joke by Harper Lee: her father was also editor of the Monroeville newspaper, so he was Atticus und Mr Underwood at the same time. → Somebody who works in the underwood of society and gradually influences opinions and attitudes.

Symbols and Metaphors

Explain the possible significance of the following symbols and metaphors that appear in the novel.

symbol	significance
black and white	
snow	
Jem's broken left arm	
the dog's madness (= rabies)	
Atticus killing the dog	
Atticus's fight against madness	
mockingbird	
Mayella's geraniums	
metaphor	*significance*
… tinfoil … winking at me in the afternoon sun …	
He began pouring out our secrets right and left.	
I should be a ray of sunshine in my father's lonely life.	
Time had slowed to a nauseating crawl.	
… walls of a pink penitentiary closing in on me …	

Symbols and Metaphors (possible answers)

symbol	significance
black and white	– white: good and innocent → pure; black: bad and guilty → corrupt – strongest possible contrast
snow	– purity – death
Jem's broken left arm	– an injury that will always be visible (will never heal completely) – parallel with Tom Robinson's crippled arm
the dog's madness (= rabies)	– people's madness raging in Maycomb
Atticus killing the dog	– although he feels pity, he has to shoot him to preserve public security – although he feels pity for Mayella Ewell, he has to immobilize her accusations in order to preserve public justice
Atticus's fight against madness	– fighting the mad dog in the street – fighting the mad mob in front of the prison – fighting the mad public opinion, prosecutor and jury by defending Tom Robinson
mockingbird	– the innocent victim (Tom Robinson; Boo Radley) – mockingbirds don't do one thing but make music for us to enjoy" (Miss Maudie) "That's why it's a sin to kill a mockingbird." – On page 200 28 Mayella says reproachfully to Atticus: "Won't answer a word you say long as you keep on mockin' me." She, too, is an innocent bird in her own way. – Braxton B. Underwood "likened Tom's death to the senseless slaughter of songbirds by hunters and children". – When Scout understands that Boo should be spared the publicity of a trial she says "Well, it'd be sort of like shootin' a mockingbird, wouldn't it?"
Mayella's geraniums	– red: symbol of passion, love – flower: symbol of growing, love, and Mayella's longing for a pretty home

metaphor	significance
… tinfoil … winking at me in the afternoon sun …	tinfoil is acting like a living person
He began pouring out our secrets right and left.	secrets are given away in great quantity and to everybody
I should be a ray of sunshine in my father's lonely life.	Scout is bright as a ray of light. This metaphor is taken up again during the description of the African M.E. church with Hunt's *The Light of the World* from 1853 showing Christ with a lantern in his hand, cf. p. 132
Time had slowed to a nauseating crawl.	Time has become a living being that can crawl.
… walls of a pink penitentiary closing in on me …	walls become something that moves, some living creature

Kopiervorlage 33.1   Flora and fauna in To Kill a Mockingbird

Flora and fauna in To Kill a Mockingbird

Make a presentation in which you make the others see the plants and animals.

page	English	German or Latin	find a picture – URL
5 33	live oak	*Lebenseiche*	http://www.netstate.com/states/symb/trees/ga_live_oak.htm
7 08	collard	*Kohl(kopf)*	Can you find a picture of a collard resembling a child's head?
7 09	rat terrier	*Kreuzung zwischen glatthaarigem Fox Terrier, Beagle und Whippet. Importrasse aus England; seit den 1930er Jahren in der gegenwärtigen Züchtungsform in den USA.*	http://quamhttp://quamut.com/quamut/rat_terriersut.com/quamut/rat_terriers
8 30	chinaberry tree	*Paternosterbaum*	find a picture
9 18	johnson grass	*Wilde Mohrenhirse (Sorghum halepense)*	http://images.harc.edu/Sites/GalvBayInvasives/Species/Photos/Thumb/SOHA_2308021.jpg
9 19	rabbit-tobacco	*Vielköpfiges Ruhrkraut (Gnaphalium polycephalum)*	http://www.opsu.edu/UnivSchools/ScienceMathNurs/PlantsGrassh/plants/pasturebig/5_24_42.jpg
9 23	azalea	*Azalee*	http://images.google.de/images?um=1&hl=de&client=opera&rls=de&q=azalea&btnG=Bilder-Suche
9 35	pecan tree	*Pekannussbaum (Carya illinoensis)*	http://www.postcardsfrom.com/gfx/txtree.gif
12 33	canna	*Canna; Indisches Blumenrohr*	find a picture
13 15	straw	*Stroh*	find pictures that show the different ways of baling straw
14 16; 102 8	squirrel	*Tamiasciurus hudsonicus;* Eichhörnchen	find a cute picture and talk about grey and red squirrels
18 24	catawba worm	caterpillars highly prized by fishermen in the Southern United States *(Köderraupe)*	http://www.ag.auburn.edu/enpl/bulletins/caterpillar/photo22.htm
21 17	hookworm	a type of parasite. [Hookworms usually enter the body through bare feet and move through the body to the small intestines where they attach thenselves with a series of hooks around their mouths.] *(Hakenwurm)*	look at this truly dramatic photo: http://scienceblogs.com/zooillogix/2007/09/hookworms_are_natures_claritin_1.php
23 06	hickory nut	a nut tree including 19 species, native to America and China *(Hickorynuss)*	
23 08	smilax	bright green twining vine, often used for Christmas decorations *(Stechwinde)*	http://www.celostnimedicina.cz/obrazky/xSmilax.jpg
23 09	turnip green	*Rübenblätter*	
25 30	butterbean	*Wachsbohne; Mondbohne; Limabohne (phaseolus lunatus)*	
31 22	toad-frog	*Krötenfrosch*	find an illustration showing *Mr. Toad* in his hall in Kenneth Graham's wonderful classic *The Wind in the Willows*, e. g. en.wikipedia.org/wiki/Mr._Toad
33 09	wistaria vine	*Glyzine; Wistarie*	find a picture of a giant blue wisteria overgrowing a pergola: http://www.kellscraft.com/AmericanGardens/americangarden15.html
39 14	camellia	a large rose-like flower growing on huge bushes *(Kamelie)*	find a picture of a white camellia
39 16	scuppernong	a sweet grape named after the Scuppernong River in northeast North Carolina *(Weintraube – amerikanische Muskatellatraubensorte)*	find a picture
47 08	nutgrass	[a tropical plant] *Cyperus papyrus (Zyperngras)*	[hated by Miss Maudie and a symbol for racism because it spreads all over once it is there]; find a picture: http://en.wikipedia.org/wiki/Cyperus

Flora and fauna in To Kill a Mockingbird

Make a presentation in which you make the others see the plants and animals.

56 02	bob-white	The Northern Bobwhite, Virginia Quail or Bobwhite Quail (Colinus virginianus) is a ground-dwelling bird native to North America. It sounds as if the bird is calling out ‚Bob White?' The bird seems sure the first name is Bob, but is asking if the last name really is White. *(Virginia-Baumwachtel)*	find a picture and listen to its sound: http://upload.wikimedia.org/wikipedia/commons/1/10/Quey_bob_white.ogg
56 09	string	an evergreen tropical plant. The leaves, dried, can be smoked. *(Hanf; Cannabis sativa)*	http://de.wikipedia.org/wiki/Hanf
56 25	kudzu	a Japanese plant (vine) [Pueraria lobata / montana / thunbergiana] *stark wuchernde Pflanze, die in den USA keine natürlichen Feinde hat.*	http://de.wikipedia.org/wiki/Kudzu_ (Pflanze)
72 31	thrift	Armeria maritime *(Grasnelke)*	find a picture
93 12	mimosa tree	(hummingbird's favourite tree) *(Mimosenbaum)*	imagine a tree full of hummingbirds – imagine the sound and the look. Can you find a photo?
99 34	bluejay	*Blauhäher* (a pretty-looking large bird that feeds on smaller oscine birds *(Singvögel)*	find a picture
99 35	mockingbird	(Mimidae, Passeriformes), American bird that copies the sounds of other birds *(Spottdrossel)*	find a picture
181 09	pilot fish	*(Naucrates ductor)* is a meat-eating fish often swimming near sharks where it eats up the shark's leftovers	find a picture of a pilot fish and his shark and then explain the metaphor given in the text
187 11	bantam cock	a tiny rooster *(Zwerghahn)*	find a picture
189 03	possum	*(didelphis)*; opossum; nocturnal (active at night) marsupial (animal carrying its offspring in a body bag) with a thick coat of hair, a long snout, and a long tail *(Beutelratte)*	find a picture that shows a possum with its long tail and talk about the context in the book where possums spread their delicious smells. Talk about Atticus being so knowledgable that he can detect a cooked possum's smell.
202 08	ground-itch	itching, caused by the entrance into the skin of the larvae of *Ancylostoma duodenale* or *Necator americanus*; hookworm disease; cf **21** *17* *(Hakenwurmkrankheit)*	
237 32	caterpillar	the larva of a butterfly, with a long soft body, many short legs, and often brightly colored or spiny skin	
262 36	roly-poly	pillbug; sowbug; *(Armadillidium vulgare)* *(gewöhnliche Rollassel)*	find a picture
262 32	lightning-bugs	firefly or glowworm. Fireflies are capable of producing a "cold light" containing no ultraviolet or infrared rays, with a wavelength from 510 to 670 nanometers, pale reddish, yellowish or green in colour, with a lighting efficiency of up to 96% *(Glühwürmchen)*	Instead of a picture, which may show a boring worm, you may come up with an artistic variety: a black night lit with millions of white little lights moving very quickly
284 31	lichen	an organism consisting of fungae and algae growing together in symbiosis that often appears on trees *(Blattflechten)*	Can you find a picture?
296 27	skunk	*(Mephitis mephitis)* mammals best known for their ability to excrete a strong, foul-smelling odor	Find a picture. In pointing out the context, explain what metaphor is used here.

Kopiervorlage 34.1 — **Legal terminology in To Kill a Mockingbird**

Legal terminology in To Kill a Mockingbird

Explain the following terms and notions. Use the glossary booklet and a dictionary. Give case examples where it seems appropriate.

	legal term	explanation	German meaning or equivalent
4 38	Code of Alabama		
4 27	read law		
5 03	second-degree murder		
5 03	plead guilty		
5 09	witness		
5 11 **194** 13; **293** 34	defence (BE; defense *today's AE*)		
5 12	first-degree murder		
5 15	criminal law		
6 25	state legislature		
11 10	probate judge		
11 10	on charges of		
11 10	disorderly conduct		
11 11	disturbing of peace		
11 12	assault and battery		
11 12	abusive language		
11 12	profane language		
11 12; **275** 26	Ladies' Law		
12 17	to charge with		
19 36	bill		
19 36	to enact		
22 32	entailment		
28 2	iniquity		
34 19	misdemeanour		
34 19	capital felony		
35 14	last-will-and-testament diction		
39 13	title		
57 6	cross-examination		
97 35	evidence		
100 27	will		
100 27	to meddle with sth.		
101 37	mortgage		

Legal terminology in To Kill a Mockingbird

Explain the following terms and notions. Use the glossary booklet and a dictionary. Give case examples where it seems appropriate.

	legal term	explanation	German meaning or equivalent
138 *24*	Blackstone's Commentaries		
149 *11*	carnal		
149 *11*	carnal knowledge		
150 *23*	penitentiary		
159, 192 *24*	defendant		
160 *09*	postponement		
176 *17*	subpoena		
179 *17*	solicitor		
179 *17*	circuit clerk		
179 *17*	judge of probate		
179 *35*	Chief Justice		
181 *21*	circuit solicitor		
181 *34*	equity		
182 *15*	deeds		
182 *20*	to throw the case out of court		
182 *22*	champertous connivance		
182 *23*	litigants		
192 *06*	contempt charge		
194 *02*	testimony		
200 *04*	state		
200 *04*	counsel		
208 *02*	contempt		
208 *33*	strict constructionist on evidence		
208 *34*	on evidence		

Legal terminology in To Kill a Mockingbird

Explain the following terms and notions. Use the glossary booklet and a dictionary. Give case examples where it seems appropriate.

	legal term	explanation	German meaning or equivalent
208 35	from the bench		
208 37	to reverse		
219 28	prosecutor		
222 29	5th Judicial Circuit Court		
223 08	corroborative evidence		
223 08	evidence		
223 09	capital charge		
223 09	indict		
224 07	to sift		
224 08	beyond all reasonable doubt		
225 14	circumstantial evidence		
225 19	to swear out a warrant		
227 08	sound		
227 10	without passion		
228 28	to acquit sb		
230 14	verdict		
235 15	appeal		
240 38	peace bond		
241 35	to go to the chair		
241 36	to commute o's sentence		
242 10	straight acquittal		
300 11	self-defence		

I, Too, Sing America

I, too, sing America.

I am the darker brother.
They send me to eat in the kitchen
When company comes,
But I laugh and eat well,
And grow strong.

Tomorrow,
I'll be at the table
When company comes.
Nobody'll dare
Say to me,
"Eat in the kitchen,"
Then.

Besides,
They'll see how beautiful I am
And be ashamed –

(Langston Hughes 1902-1967)

© 1994 by The Estate of Langston Hughes published by permission of Harold Ober Associates, New York

Students A:
Can you "summarise" a poem? – Try and describe what is said in the poem in German to somebody who doesn't speak English.

Students B:
Is it possible to recreate the effect of the poem in a different language? – Try and write a German/ … translation of the poem.

Students C:
What is so bad about eating in the kitchen? – Explain why the person in the poem does not want to eat in the kitchen in future.

Students D:
Is the author realistic about the future of the African Americans? – The poem was written in 1926. Evaluate the author's view of the future of the African Americans that he puts forward in this poem.

Students E:
What effect does the form of the poem have on the reader? – Analyse the poetic devices (images, metaphors) (A.-bereich II) and comment on the effect that the short lines have on the reader.

Harlem

What happens to a dream deferred?

Does it dry up
like a raisin in the sun?
Or fester like a sore –
And then run?
Does it stink like rotten meat?
Or crust and sugar over –
like a syrupy sweet?

Maybe it just sags
like a heavy load.

Or does it explode?

(Langston Hughes 1902-1967)

© 1994 by The Estate of Langston Hughes published by permission of Harold Ober Associates, New York

---

[1] **to defer** to delay sth until a later time
[2] **raisin** Rosine
[3] **to fester** to become badly infected
[4] **sore** painful wound
[5] **rotten** decayed and no longer edible
[6] **to sag** to hang down in the middle because of weight

Harlem – form, similes, topic

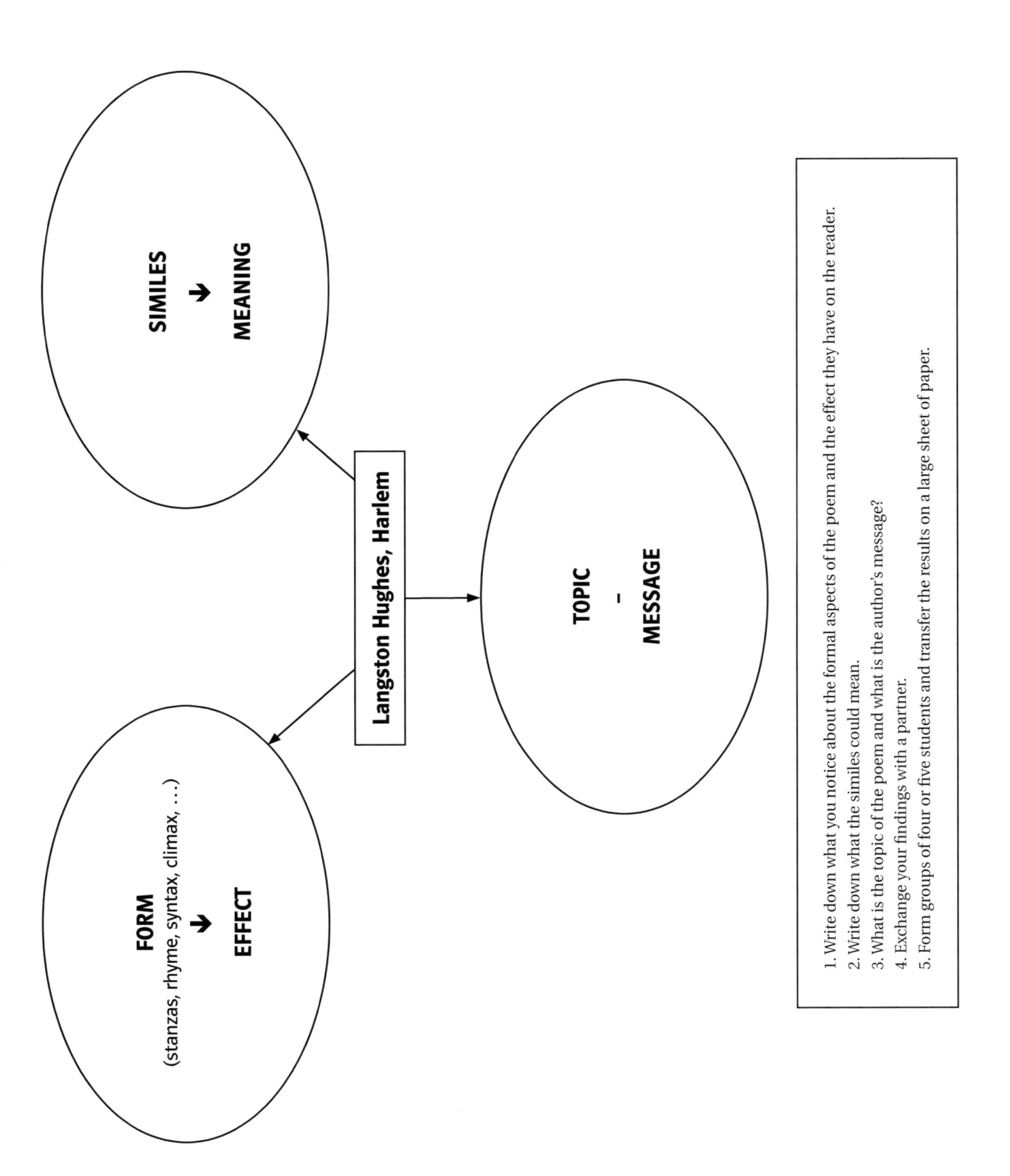

Kopiervorlage 35.3

Langston Hughes, Harlem

- SIMILES → MEANING
- TOPIC – MESSAGE
- FORM (stanzas, rhyme, syntax, climax, …) → EFFECT

1. Write down what you notice about the formal aspects of the poem and the effect they have on the reader.
2. Write down what the similes could mean.
3. What is the topic of the poem and what is the author's message?
4. Exchange your findings with a partner.
5. Form groups of four or five students and transfer the results on a large sheet of paper.

Class Test A

EMMA TAYLOR, 89, was born a slave of the Greer family, in Mississippi. She and her mother were sold to a Texas man, whose name Emma has forgotten. Emma lives with one of her children, in Tyler, Texas. In 1936, she tells the story of her life.

"My maw and paw lived in Mississippi, and belonged to Marse Greer. Dat dere name, too. All the slaves token dere master's name, 'cause day hadn't no use for a name, nohow.

"De first thing I 'members is followin' my maw in the cotton patch. She allus went ahead, pickin' cotton, and made a clean place with her sack draggin' on the ground. But de first work I ever done was feed de
5 chickens and geese and shell corn to feed dem.

"Us nigger chillen couldn't play with de white chillen. De worstest whippin' I ever got was for playin' with a doll what belonged to one marse's chillen. I 'members it yet and I ain't never seed a doll purty as dat doll was to me. It was make out a corncob with arms and legs what moved and a real head, with eyes and hair and mouth painted on. It had a dress out of silk cloth, jist like one my missus weared when she went to
10 meetin'. Dat li'l gal done leave de doll under de tree, but missus found me playin' with it and whipped me hard.

"We lived in a cabin in de back field 'hind de big house, one room and a shed room, where maw done all de cookin' for de whole family. I had three brothers and three sisters, all dead, I supposes. Dey all older'n what I was. We cooked on a fireplace, and a big pot hanged on poles over de fire and de bread cook on
15 dat fire in a skillet what was made of two pieces of iron, turn up all round. We puts de dough in one and turns de other one over it, den buries it in de coals a few minutes till it brown on de top and bottom. It was good, jist as good as nowadays, baked in an oven. Our beds was made out of straw and ol' rags, but we kept warm sleepin' a whole lot in one bed in winter, but we slept outside in summer.

"I was sold one time. Marse, he gittin' old and 'cide he didn't need so many slaves, so he have de sale and
20 a man come and put us all up on a big platform. We pulls off nearly all our clothes, so as to show how big we was, and he 'gins hollerin' 'bout who gwineter buy, who gwineter buy. I was scart and thunk I has to leave maw, so I 'gins hollerin' jist as loud as he does. He turn 'round and say, 'Shut up, you li'l coon, you, I can't hear nothin'.' I hides my face in maw's apron and didn't know no more till we's all loaded in a wagon and starts to de new home. We gits dere and is give new clothes and shoes, de first ones I ever had on and
25 it taken me a long time to larn to wear dem things on my feet.

"Us niggers has to git up at four in de mornin', and work, work till us can't see no more. Den dey work at night. De men chops wood and hauls poles to build fences and make wood, and de women folks has to spin four cuts of thread every night and make all de clothes. Some has to card cotton to make quilts and some weave and knits stockin's. Marse give each one a chore to do at night and iffen it warn't did when we
30 went to bed, we's whipped. One time I falls pumb asleep befo' I finishes shellin' some corn, but I didn't git a bad whippin' dat time.

"Sometimes de niggers danced and played de fiddle and us chillen played in de yard. We could stay up all night. Dat during' harvest or at Christmas time.

"All de victuals was issued out by de overseer and he give 'nough for one week, den iffen us eat it all up too
35 soon, it am jist go without. Lots of times, I went down to de 'tato patch a long time after everybody am in bed, and stole 'tatoes, so we wouldn't be hungry next day. I allus covered de hoe up good and never did git cotched. De dogs got after me one time, but I put pepper in day eyes and dey stopped. I allus carried peper with me.

"I marries when I'm fifteen, not so long befo' I'm free. Nigger men didn't git no license to marry day gals
40 den. Dey jist picked her out and asked mares, and iffen he 'grees, day's married. But iffen he don't want it, dat man has to find heself 'nother gal. De men what lived on 'nother plantation couldn't see dare wives but onct every two weeks. Marse buyed my husban', Rube Taylor, and he come to live with me.

---

7 **purty** pretty
9 **cloth** material *Stoff*
29 **chore** task

"One day marse say we's all free and we has a big celebration, eatin' and dancin'. But we near all stayed on his place for a long time after day. He paid us thirty-five cents de day and let us live in de same old houses.

"After we done left him, we jist drifts 'round, workin' for white folks, till we manages to git a farm. Rube done died a long time back, and I lives with my baby child." *(892 words)*

***

Ex-Slave Story (Texas) from: Slave Narratives from the Federal Writers' Project, 1936-1938, pp 73-75 of 237, http://memory.loc.gov/cgi-bin/ampage

Tasks

1. Language A

Translate the slang words into Standard English

1. allus _____
2. 'coon _____
3. dare _____
4. dat _____
5. de worstest _____
6. done leave _____
7. gal _____
8. git cotched _____
9. gwineter _____
10. hoe _____
11. iffen _____
12. jist _____
13. li'l _____
14. Marse _____
15. members _____
16. 'nough _____
17. scart _____
18. 'tato _____
19. thunk _____
20. weren't did _____

Master – just – if – little – girl – their – heap – potato – had left – the worst – going to – scared – thought – get caught – always – thought – racoon – it it wasn't done – that – enough – remember

2. Language B

Write a headline for each paragraph

3. Comprehension (70-90 words each)

1. Retell the incident of the third paragraph (11-21) in your own words, starting with "I".
2. Describe how the family lived, slept, and cooked.

4. Analysis

Explain in which way the presentation of Emma Taylor's history differs from the way black people's lives are portrayed in *To Kill a Mockingbird, Uncle Tom's Cabin* or *The Adventures of Huckleberry Finn*? – How does this affect the reader? Compare the differences.

5a. Comment

Discuss the idea to collect ex-slave stories (in the case of the USA) or war-stories or other so called grassroots history tales *("Geschichte von unten")*. Is it a way to see history in a different light? Does it really cast a different light on world history?

5b. Creation of Text

Write a letter to the Library of Congress in which you explain how the recorded history of Emma Taylor affected you. Express your gratitude for making these documents available online and point out how important it is to have original documents from the people concerned, not just professional writers. State the importance of those anonymous people having their voice heard and assess its meaning for a functioning democracy. Finish your letter by expressing the hope that the *Deutsche Nationalbibliothek* in Berlin, Leipzig and Frankfurt will start a similar project, preserving the tales of old people from a different cultural background who live in Germany now – and you want to be the person to record them.

Lösungsskizze Klausur A

1. Language A

1. always; 2. racoon; 3. their; 4. that; 5. the worst; 6. has left; 7. girl; 8. get caught; 9. going to; 10. heap; 11. if; 12. just; 13. little; 14. Master; 15. remember; 16. enough; 17. scared; 18. potato; 19. thought; 20. wasn't done

2. Language B

Emma's parents and master; first memories of her cotton-picking mother, first work; playing with a white girl's doll; house, cooking, and sleeping; being sold; men's and women's chores; celebrating; not enough food; getting married; getting free; life after slavery

3. Comprehension

1. I received my worst whipping when I played with the doll of a little white girl. I had never seen such a pretty doll. It was made out of a corncob, its arms and legs moved and it had a real head with eyes, hair and a mouth painted on. The little girl had left her doll under a tree, and when missus found me playing with it she whipped me badly.
2. The family – father, mother, and seven children – lived in one cabin and a shed. In winter, they all slept in beds made of straw and rags, often keeping warm by sleeping all in one bed. In summer, they slept outside. Her mother did the cooking in the shed over an open fireplace in a big pot hanging on poles over the fire. She did her baking on a skillet made of two pieces of iron. The children liked her cooking very much.

4. Analysis

The main difference is the point of view of the narrator. All other histories are seen from the outside – this is a story told from personal experience. The result is authenticity. The reader is put into the shoes of the little slave girl. One almost feels the physical pain of being whipped just for doing the most natural things – playing with a doll. – A feeling of injustice is instilled in the reader, of protest and great sorrow for the girl who represents many generations of slaves. – In *To Kill a Mockingbird* blacks are seen from the outside, from Scout's point of view, though friendly. She praises the good smells of their cooking, their singing and praying and caring for each other at church, and characterizes a very civilized community, but the point of view is that of a girl with as yet little experience. – In *Uncle Tom* an educated white lady takes the point of view of various black people, mainly Uncle Tom. Yet there is a difference in authenticity between the highly erudite text of Beecher-Stowe and Emma Taylor. One never forgets one is reading a novel, not a real life history. – In *Huck Finn* the *nigger Jim* is a friend on the same level as Huck, yet his history, too, is seen and described from the outside. The reader is always in Huck's skin. The way Huck sees Jim changes when they start travelling together. Before, Jim is hardly more than a "human chattle" – Huck's usual perspective of slaves –, but when Huck discovers they are in the same situation he starts seeing him as a fellow human being. However, we never really understand how Jim feels.

5a Evaluation: Comment

Arguments supporting the idea to collect ex-slave stories:
- nobody was able to tell their stories the way they could themselves
- the language is authentic, though not standard American
- the grammar is different but authentic
- the structure in which the stories are told is different: basic survival plays a large role
- personal examples say more about the real impact of slavery than long sociological essays, e.g. the episode of the little girl Emma Taylor who is whipped for playing with a doll which was made out of a corn cob
- a reader can begin to imagine today what it must be like to be somebody elses property.
- selling situation is similar: very authentic, one still feels the fear of being separated from the mother
- only 10 or 20 years later these witnesses would not have been available any more; their voices would have been dead for all times
- The Simon Wiesenthal Center in Los Angeles tries a similar project: collecting memories of people who died in the Holocaust.
- Steven Spielberg picked up the idea, too, 1994: Survivors of the Shoah Visual History Foundation also collects authentic interviews with survivors.

Are there arguments against it?

Only people who treated slaves like objects and work machines or even today do not see them as human beings could argue against the importance of the collected stories.

Conclusion:

- grassroot history is very important in order to understand what really went on in history
- one has to find the "slaves" of each period and write their history

Class Test B

Barack Obama, Victory Speech November 4, 2008 (abbr.)

Hello Chicago,

If there is anyone out there who still doubts that America is a place where all things are possible; who still wonders if the dream of our founders is alive in our time; who still questions the power of our democracy, tonight is your answer.

It's the answer spoken by young and old, rich and poor, Democrat and Republican, black, white, Latino,
5 Asian, Native American, gay, straight, disabled and not disabled – Americans who sent a message to the world that we have never been a collection of Red States and Blue States: we are, and always will be, the United States of America.

It's been a long time coming, but tonight, because of what we did on this day, in this election, at this defining moment, change has come to America.

10 I was never the likeliest candidate for this office. We didn't start with much money or many endorsements. Our campaign was built by working men and women who dug into what little savings they had to give five dollars and ten dollars and twenty dollars to this cause. It grew strength from the millions of Americans who volunteered, and organized, and proved that more than two centuries later, a government of the people, by the people and for the people has not perished from this Earth. This is your victory.

15 I know you didn't do this just to win an election and I know you didn't do it for me. You did it because you understand the enormity of the task that lies ahead. For even as we celebrate tonight, we know the challenges that tomorrow will bring are the greatest of our lifetime - two wars, a planet in peril, the worst financial crisis in a century.

So let us summon a new spirit of patriotism; of service and responsibility where each of us resolves to pitch
20 in and work harder and look after not only ourselves, but each other.

Let us resist the temptation to fall back on the same partisanship and pettiness and immaturity that has poisoned our politics for so long.

This election had many firsts and many stories that will be told for generations. But one that's on my mind tonight is about a woman who cast her ballot in Atlanta. She's a lot like the millions of others who stood in
25 line to make their voice heard in this election except for one thing – Ann Nixon Cooper is 106 years old.

She was born just a generation past slavery; a time when there were no cars on the road or planes in the sky; when someone like her couldn't vote for two reasons – because she was a woman and because of the color of her skin.

And tonight, I think about all that she's seen throughout her century in America – the heartache and the
30 hope; the struggle and the progress; the times we were told that we can't, and the people who pressed on with that American creed: Yes we can.

At a time when women's voices were silenced and their hopes dismissed, she lived to see them stand up and speak out and reach for the ballot. Yes we can.

When there was despair in the dust bowl and depression across the land, she saw a nation conquer fear
35 itself with a New Deal, new jobs and a new sense of common purpose. Yes we can.

When the bombs fell on our harbor and tyranny threatened the world, she was there to witness a generation rise to greatness and a democracy was saved. Yes we can.

She was there for the buses in Montgomery, the hoses in Birmingham, a bridge in Selma, and a preacher from Atlanta who told a people that We Shall Overcome. Yes we can.

40 A man touched down on the moon, a wall came down in Berlin, a world was connected by our own science and imagination. And this year, in this election, she touched her finger to a screen, and cast her vote, because after 106 years in America, through the best of times and the darkest of hours, she knows how America can change. Yes we can.

America, we have come so far. We have seen so much. But there is so much more to do. So tonight, let us
45 ask ourselves - if our children should live to see the next century; if my daughters should be so lucky to live as long as Ann Nixon Cooper, what change will they see? What progress will we have made?

This is our chance to answer that call. This is our moment. This is our time - to put our people back to work and open doors of opportunity for our kids; to restore prosperity and promote the cause of peace; to reclaim the American Dream and reaffirm that fundamental truth - that out of many, we are one; that while
50 we breathe, we hope, and where we are met with cynicism, and doubt, and those who tell us that we cant, we will respond with that timeless creed that sums up the spirit of a people:

Yes We Can. Thank you, God bless you, and may God Bless the United States of America.

Klausur B

Tasks

1. Language A
Match the words and phrases with the definitions

1. campaign (_)
2. cast her ballott (_)
3. perished (_)
4. generation (_)
5. slavery (_)
6. struggle (_)
7. tyranny (_)
8. hoses (_)
9. reclaim (_)
10. challenges (_)

definitions

A state of a person who is a chattel of another person
B a stimulating task or problem
C a government which gives absolute power to its ruler
D series of operations to win an election
E group of individuals born and living at the same time
F restore from an undesirable state
G disappeared
H flexible tubes used to spray water from fire engines
I voted
J fight in order to solve a problem or change a situation

2. Language B

a) 'So let us summon a new spirit of patriotism; of service and responsibility'. – Explain.

_____

b) Where we are met with cynicism, and doubt, and those who tell us that we can't, we will respond with that timeless creed that sums up the spirit of a people: Yes We Can. Rephrase.

_____
_____
_____
_____
_____

c) timeless creed – give a synonym

_____

3. Comprehension (50-70 words each)

1. When the bombs fell on our harbor and tyranny threatened the world, she was there to witness a generation rise to greatness, and a democracy was saved. – Explain these allusions.

2. A man touched down on the moon, a wall came down in Berlin, a world was connected by our own science and imagination. – What is the role of America in these three allusions? Give a critical account of its implications.

4. Comment (150 words)

Analyse Obama's speech and its rhetorical elements putting particular emphasis on the role of Ann Nixon Cooper. Why and for which purpuose did he choose her? – Comment on the aim of the speech and put it into its historical perspective.

Lösungsskizze Klausur B

1. Language A

1 1D, 2I, 3G, 4E, 5A, 6J, 7C, 8H, 9F, 10 B

2. Language B

a) Let us command a new kind of patriotism / We require a new kind of patriotism
b) To people who treat us cynically and doubtfully, and to others who keep telling us that we do nothing right or not at all we will say, as generations before us have said, Yes, We Can. We can do it right. And we will do it.
c) classic, time-honoured, well-established, everlasting, eternal, indestructable – idea, opinion, view, conviction, belief, credo, principle

3. Comprehension

1. Obama refers to the bombing of Pearl Harbour on December 7, 1941 which marked the beginning of World War II for the United States; Americans "rose to greatness" in their fight agains Hitler – Mussolini tyrannies and saved the American democracy.
2. It is a reference to three political occurrences in which America was first in world history: on July 20, 1969, Apollo 11 was the first human vehicle to reach the moon, and Neil Armstrong was the first human being to touch the moon. Although the Russians had been the first to send men into orbit (and return them alive), Americans like to stress that it was one of them who first touched down on the moon. When the Berlin Wall came down in 1989, dividing the Eastern and the Western Block, it seemed again that the Western – the American influenced – world had won a victory (not considering people's fights for freedom and the economic breakdown of the system). And finally, the world wide web, though first established at CERN in Geneva, Switzerland, is claimed to be the invention of American science and imagination.

4. Comment

Anne Nixon Cooper is used as a personification of America's Progress. O. refers to the constitutional rights of freedom and equality and uses her to show the historical progress made in the last 106 years. By following her curriculum vitae, he answers the questions "How has America changed during her lifetime? Which changes has America undergone?" (no votes for women; no votes for blacks; slavery abolished just 25 years ago; cars and planes not in use; Great Depression and Roosevelt's New deal; World War II – Pearl Harbour – Hitler's tyrany; Civil Rights' Movement in the 1960s with the events: bus boycott in Montgomery; firehoses in Birmingham hit high school demonstrators for Civil Rights; in 1965, 600 participants started out on a march from Selma, Alabama to the capital Montgomery in order to register as voters; the march was bludgeoned; http://www.youtube.com/watch?v=s00-OoZAWno Martin Luther King repeated it with great success; 1969: first landing on the moon; 1989: Berlin Wall came down, marking the end of the Cold War, www connects the world; in this election people can vote by touching a screen with a finger). The Civil Rights Movement has come to "cash its check" with Obama being US-President.

rhetorical elements

alliterations (much money or many; planet in peril; summon a new spirit; partisanship and pettiness, poisoned politics; heartache and the hope; times we were told; people who pressed; stand up and speak; despair in the dust bowl; generation greatness; buses – Birmingham – bridge; put our people; open doors of opportunity; prosperity and promote; reclaim and reaffirm; sums up the spirit. [very musical effect]
allusions, combined with *ellipses* since the actual political event is not mentioned by name (dream of our founders – Bill of Rights 1789; Red States – states won by Republicans and Blue States – states won by Democrats; government of the people, by the people and for the people has not perished - November 19th, 1863, closing phrase of Gettysburg Address by Abraham Lincoln; two wars – one in Iraq and one in Afghanistan; planet in peril – United Nations Framework Convention on Climate Change, (UNFCCC) to limit the greenhouse gas emissions; financial crisis – crisis in America and worldwide since 2008; stood in line – Americans formed long queues in order to vote, often waiting their turn for two and more hours; despair in the dust bowl – erosion in the Great Plains, 1935-1938; depression across the land – 1929-1941 great economic crisis; conquer fear itself with a New Deal – Roosevelt's economic programme, words from his inaugural address; bombs fell on our harbour – December 7, 1941, military strike by Japanese navy against US naval base at Pearl Harbor, Hawaii, resulting in the US becoming militarily involved in World War II; tyranny threatened the world – Nazi Germany fought a World War; Generation rise to greatness – 1968 freedom marches; buses in Montgomery – Rosa Parks declined to get up from a bus seat for white people December 1, 1955 in Montgomery, Alabama; hoses in Birmingham – MLK's non-violent campaign for Civil Rights in Birmingham, Alabama which got out of hand. It was a major factor in the national push towards the Civil Rights Act of 1964,

which prohibited racial discrimination in hiring practices and public services in the United States; bridge in Selma – s. o.; a preacher from Atlanta – MLK; We Shall Overcome – a protest song that became a key anthem for the Civil Rights Movement; a man touched down on the moon – July 20, 1969, when the American Astronaut Neil Armstrong first set foot on the surface of the moon; a wall came down in Berlin – November 9, 1989; world was connected – 1958 the beginning of the internet by the setup of ARPA (Advanced Research Projects Agency); out of many, we are one – E pluribus unum – motto on the 1776 seal of United States, now on 1-dollar-bill, considered a de-facto-motto of the United States, to be seen in the National emblem in the US).
parallelisms: no cars on the road or planes in the sky; the heartache and the hope; the struggle and the progress; when women's voices were silenced and their hopes dismissed; stand up and speak out and reach for the ballot; despair in the dust bowl and depression across the land ; a New Deal, no jobs and a new sense of common purpose; buses in Montgomery, houses in Birmingham, a bridge in Selma, and a preacher from Atlanta; a man touched down on the moon, a wall came down in Berlin; And this year, in this election; through the best of times and the darkest of hours; we have come so far. We have seen so much; to put our people back to work and open doors of opportunity for our kids; to restore prosperity and promote the cause of peace; to reclaim the American Dream and reaffirm that fundamental truth; that out of many, we are one; that while we breathe, we hope.
climax: government of the people, by the people and for the people – This is our chance to answer that call. This is our moment. This is our time. –
anaphora Yes, we can.
rhythm the parallelisms carry a strong rhythm that features the whole speech
appeal to the listener Obama addresses the listeners directly, using *you* a lot: tonight is your answer; God bless you. He includes the listener throughout the speech, using *we* and *our*.
general impression He makes this victory not one of personal merit but outlines his function as a president as a service. He has a vocation to fulfill in regard to the American Constitution. He outlines a historical development that implicitly he intends to continue improving. But he never speaks for himself, he only depicts himself as mirroring his audience. – He smiles a lot and is generally relaxed while speaking. His voice is melodious but not styled to sound black; the rhythm of his speech sounds melodic and the speech itself sounds improvised. He does not read it off a sheet. He looks at his audience while speaking, never at a script.
[Comment: When she was born in 1902, slavery had just been abolished for a little over a generation, 1865. Although the American Constitution had guaranteed that "all men are created equal" people of different colour of skin were treated very differently. An added inhibition was the fact that she was a woman who had no vote at that time, no matter if black or white. So in reality a woman at that time lived with very few fundamental rights, contrary to the constitution. But there were women like the suffragettes who fought for votes for women in New York in 1912 because they wanted this dream to come true that all persons are created equal. Even though men tried to silence their voices, they believed in equal rights. Anne Nixon Cooper witnessed the Great Depression with millions of people unemployed. She was there when the states of Texas, New Mexico, Oklahoma, Colorado und Kansas were turned into "dust bowls" from years of heat and harsh winds, making more than 3 million farmers leave their homes. She was there when Roosevelt said in his Inaugural Address that America had "nothing to fear but fear itself" which was his way of trying to encourage his people. These words are mentioned in *To Kill A Mockingbird* merely as an allusion, but they are there as a quote 6 9. Ann Nixon Cooper survived with many others who got new jobs thanks to Roosevelt's politics of New Deal. She was there in the racial uproars in 1968 which started with Rosa Parks and the Montgomery Bus Boycott when a black lady would not sit in the "black section" of a public bus. She was around when Martin Luther King, a black preacher from Atlanta, made his legendary speech for 250,000 Americans in Washington in which he sketched his dream of white and black children holding hands – one day. Shortly afterwards, he was killed. But the song of that march, "We shall overcome", has endured, and he was made a martyr and a hero rather than silenced by his death. Anne Nixon Cooper witnessed the first landing on the moon, the end of the Berlin Wall – a symbol of the Iron Curtain that devided the Eastern and the Western Sphere –, and the world wide web to come into existence – symbols of peace and understanding and expansion into the universe. Perhaps her great-grandchildren will see even more justice, the end of the wars in Iraq and Afghanistan, and financial prosperity in the world.]
Why is this speech so fascinating? Because it addresses the American people as one body, rather than individuals; Obama reconstructs the one world of ideas that once helped to form this state and the common tasks that derive from it; he focuses on the individuals *conglomerating* into one political body in simple language. He generates a feeling of belonging. He finds a modern synonym for *home and patriotism.* He renews Lincoln's address of patriotism and MLK's sueing for Civil Rights in modern language and an amount of sentimentality that is just this side of kitsch.

Literatur

Castleman, Tamara ShellineNotes™ Lee's *To Kill a Mockingbird*. 99 pages, IDG Books Worldwide, Chicago, Indianapolis, New York 2000. Auch online verfügbar unter http://education.yahoo.com/homework_help/cliffsnotes/to_kill_a_mockingbird/

Milton, Joyce, Harper Lee's *To Kill A Mockingbird*. 100 pages, Barron's Book Notes, Barron's Educational Series, New York 1984

Monroe County Heritage Museum, Images of America. Monroeville. TheSearch for Harper Lee's Maycomb. 128 pages, Arcadia Publishing, Charleston SC, Chicago IL, Portsmouth NH, San Francisco CA 1999

Robbins, Mari Lu, M.A., A Guide for Using *To Kill a Mockingbird* in the Classroom. Based on the novel written by Harper Lee. 48 pages, Teacher Created Resources, Westminster CA, 2007

Schede, Hans-Georg, Erläuterungen zu Harper Lee *To Kill a Mockingbird*. 120 S., Königs Erläuterungen und Materialien, Band 478. Bange Verlag 2008, Hollfeld

Sims, Beth, To Kill a Mockingbird. Harper Lee. 87 pages, York Press, London 2002

Von den unzählbaren Websites seien hier einige aufgeführt, die sich gut für die Verwendung im Unterricht eignen:

http://www.gradesaver.com/classicnotes/quiz/killmockingbird/1/ (Abschnittsweise multiple-choice-Fragen zum Inhalt jedes Kapitels).

http://www.lorenwebster.net/In_a_Dark_Time/category/longer-works/to-kill-a-mockingbird Ein Diskussionsforum zu einzelnen Zitaten aus dem Buch, die ausführlich analysiert werden. Dies kann zur erweiterten Diskussion im Unterricht herangezogen werden.

http://en.wikipedia.org/wiki/List_of_characters_in_To_Kill_a_Mockingbird#Maudie_Atkinson Umfangreiche Einzelcharakterisierung der Haupt- und Nebenpersonen.

http://en.wikipedia.org/wiki/Nehi. Wer Spaß daran hat, sich in die kleinsten Details zu vertiefen: Nehi Cola, das in den Prozesspausen getrunken wird, gibt es wirklich.

http://www.funtrivia.com/en/Literature/Lee-Harper-8934.html Questions, facts, and information on the book.

http://www.swisseduc.ch/english/readinglist/lee_harper/mockingbird/index.html Weitere Aufgaben, Zusammenfassungen unc Interpretationen zum Roman.

http://research.education.purdue.edu/challenge/webquest/2001_2002/Wolcott/processl.htm Die Unterrichtseinheit einer amerikanischen Lehrerin, in der mit Hilfe von Internet-Links individuelle Aufgaben zum politischen Hintergrund gegeben und bewertet werden. Aufwändig, aber für die Schüler sehr gewinnbringend.

http://www.tokillamockingbird.com/ ist die Homepage des Monroe County Heritage Museums. Dort kann man viele Originalschauplätze des Romans im Bild betrachten. (Monroeville = Maycomb)

http://www.loc.gov/rr/print/list/085_disc.html Auf dieser Photostrecke der Library of Congress sind 31 schwarz-weiße Meisterphotographien abgebildet, die Rassendiskriminierung im Süden der USA in den 30er Jahren dokumentieren.

http://www.lausd.k12.ca.us/Belmont_HS/tkm/ enthält neben Worterklärungen und Erläuterungen verdeckter Zitate ("allusions") wunderbares Bildmaterial, das Kapitel für Kapitel herausgesucht wurde und sehr gut im Unterricht eingesetzt werden kann.

http://www.pbs.org/wgbh/amex/scottsboro/maps/index.html Details zum Scottsboro-Prozess: Film, Timeline, Infos, Unterrichtsmaterial (Vorlage für den Robinson-Prozess).